Simple Weather Experiments With Everyday Materials

Muriel Mandell

Illustrated by Frances Zweifel

Sterling Publishing Co., Inc.   New York

Acknowledgments:

The author wishes to thank the following for their suggestions: John Kaminski, Assistant Director of the Science Unit of the New York City Board of Education; Dr. Lloyd Motz, Professor Emeritus of Columbia University; Dr. Betty Rosoff, Professor Emeritus of Stern College; and, of course, my editor, Sheila Barry.

Library of Congress Cataloging-in-Publication Data

Mandell, Muriel.
    Simple weather experiments with everyday materials / by Muriel Mandell ;
illustrated by Frances Zweifel.
        p.   cm.
    Includes index.
    Summary: Presents over sixty experiments exploring the mysteries
of climate and weather.
    1. Weather—Experiments—Juvenile literature.   2. Climatology—
Experiments—Juvenile literature.   [1. Weather—Experiments.
2. Climatology—Experiments.   3. Experiments.]   I. Zweifel, Frances
W., ill.   II. Title.
QC981.3.M36   1990
551.5'078—dc20   90-37915
                                                         CIP
                                                          AC

First paperback edition published in 1991 by
Sterling Publishing Company, Inc.
387 Park Avenue South, New York, N.Y. 10016
© 1990 by Muriel Mandell
Distributed in Canada by Sterling Publishing
% Canadian Manda Group, P.O. Box 920, Station U
Toronto, Ontario, Canada M8Z 5P9
Distributed in Great Britain and Europe by Cassell PLC
Villiers House, 41/47 Strand, London WC2N 5JE, England
Distributed in Australia by Capricorn Ltd.
P.O. Box 665, Lane Cove, NSW 2066
Manufactured in the United States of America
All rights reserved

Sterling ISBN 0-8069-7296-3   Trade
               0-8069-7295-5   Paper

For Jean and Aviva

CONTENTS

Before You Begin   6

Warming Up   8

Earth's Temperature Records • What Warms Us? •
About the Sun • Heat Wave • Why Is Spring
Sometimes Late? • Black, White, and Shiny • Let It
Snow • Land vs. Water • Water vs. Air • Time in
the Sun • Why Is Summer Hotter Than Winter? •
Why Is the Equator Hotter Than the North Pole? •
Shadow Thermometer • Length vs. Height • The
House Is Moving! • Does the Sun Rise in the
Morning? • Catching Up • Foucault's Pendulum •
Why We See the Sun After It "Sets" • As the World
Turns • Sun in Your Room • Why Do We Have
Seasons? • Making an Ellipse • The Greenhouse
Effect

Whirling Winds and Gentle Breezes   40

Earth's Wind Records • Earth's Atmosphere • Air
Takes Up Space • Air Has Weight • A Lot of Hot Air
• Air Currents and Wind • How Much Oxygen Is in
the Air? • What Causes an Air Inversion? • Is Your
Air Polluted? • Prevailing Winds • Whirling Winds
• Local Winds • Air Masses and Fronts • Air
Pressure and Weather Prediction • A Trick Can •
Ballot's Law • Tornado! • Bernoulli's Law • More
About Tornadoes • Eye of a Hurricane

Water, Water, Everywhere   68

Earth's Precipitation Records • Water Going Into the Air • Evaporation Race #1 • Wind and Water • Evaporation Race #2 • Evaporation Cools Air • Water Coming Out of the Air • Indoor Cloud • Why Clouds Look White • Be a Rain Maker! • Measuring the Size of a Raindrop • What Causes Smog? • Ozone • Refrigerator Weather • Dissecting a Hailstone • What Is Lightning? • Does Lightning Ever Strike Twice in the Same Spot? • Storm Warnings • What Causes Thunder? • How Far Away Is the Storm? • Make Your Own Rainbow

Building a Weather Station   94

Keeping Records • Straw Thermometer • Temperature Conversion • Reading a Barometer • Bottle Barometer • Balloon Barometer • Weather Vane • Cup Anemometer • The Beaufort Scale • How Cold Do You Feel? • Milk Carton Hygrometer • Relative Humidity Table • How Hot Do You Feel? • How Uncomfortable Do You Feel? • Dew Point • Rain Gauge • Reading the Clouds • Cloud Chart • pH Scale • Acid Rain

Weather Glossary   125

Index   127

Before You Begin

Why is the North Pole colder than the equator? Why does the Sun set? What causes thunder and lightning?

From experiments in this book, you'll find out about these and many other mysteries of climate and weather.

Climate is the average weather of a region over a long period. Weather has to do with daily changes in the lower part of the atmosphere—the ocean of air that surrounds the Earth.

Both climate and weather are created by the interaction of the Earth and the Sun. Both climate and weather have to do with warmth, wind, and water. The experiments here all explore how and why.

You'll discover why some places and some parts of the year are warmer than others. You may be surprised to know that closeness to the Sun is *not* the reason!

You'll find out what creates wind and why it sometimes is so destructive. You'll learn why cold air usually brings "high pressure" and good weather, while warm air often causes "low pressure," bad weather and strong winds.

You'll come to understand snow, sleet and hail, lightning and thunder.

You'll be able to make your own weather station, putting together the instruments you need to keep track of temperature, air pressure, wind direction and speed, humidity and rainfall.

You can start with any experiment in any chapter, but you'll get the most out of this book if you take one chapter at a time and do most of the experiments in order.

In a few of the experiments, you'll need to use a safety match or a stove, and these are labelled HOT! You can see them at a glance and get help, if that's the rule at your house.

Some of these experiments are great tricks that you can use to amaze yourself and your friends. But the best part is that they give you hands-on experiences that show the scientific principles behind weather, so that you can understand them— from the ground up.

WARMING UP

What heats our Earth? Why are some places warm and some cold? Why do we have tropical deserts near the equator and the frozen tundras at the poles? What causes the seasons? What is the "greenhouse effect"?

Perform the simple experiments in this chapter and discover the answers to these questions—and others!

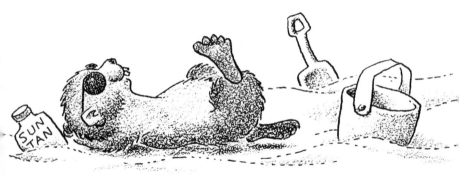

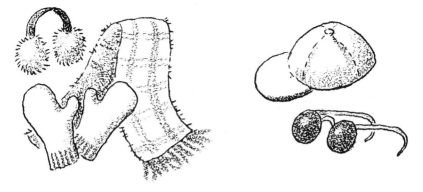

EARTH'S TEMPERATURE RECORDS

Highest temperature: 136°F (57.7°C)
Place: Azizia, Tripolitania, Libya
Date: September 13, 1922
Longest hot spell: 100°F (38°C) for 162 consecutive days
Place: Martin Bar, Western Australia
Date: October 31, 1923–April 7, 1924
Highest annual mean temperature: 94°F (34.4°C)
Place: Dallol, Ethiopia
Date: 1960–1966
Hottest hot spell: 120°F (48.8°C) or more for 43 consecutive days
Place: Death Valley, California
Date: July 6–August 17, 1917
Lowest temperature: −129°F (−89°C)
Place: Vostok, Antarctica
Date: July 21, 1983
Lowest temperature in an inhabited place: −90.4°F (−68°C)
Place: Oymyakon, Siberia, USSR
Date: Feb. 3, 1933
Lowest recorded annual mean temperature: −70°F (−56.6°C)
Place: Pleasteau Station, Antarctica

9

What Warms Us?

Indoors, we use coal, oil, gas, or electricity to heat and light our homes and workplaces. But what provides the heat and light outdoors? What warms the Earth and the objects on it?

You need:
a sunny window

What to do:
On a sunny day, hold one hand up behind a shaded window. Lift the shade or blind. Now hold your hand up to the window again.

What happens:
Instantly, the hand in the Sun feels warmer.

Why:
You didn't touch anything but you felt the heat. It came from the Sun—a star 93 million miles away from Earth.

Like all stars, the Sun is a great ball of hot gases that pours out huge amounts of heat and light and other energy. Only a tiny part of that energy reaches us. But it is enough to light and warm the Earth.

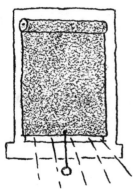 

ABOUT THE SUN

The Sun is a medium-sized star—a huge, hot ball of gas. It is one among billions in the galaxy, the same family of stars. Though it varies from 90 million miles away in winter to 96 million miles away in summer (144 to 153.6 million km), it is still the closest star to Earth.

The Sun measures 864,000 miles (1,400,000 km) across—108 times larger than Earth.

The Sun makes its own light and heat—and provides the light and heat for the Earth—by a process that is similar to what happens in the hydrogen bomb.

The Sun's extreme heat (millions of degrees at the center) causes its hydrogen atoms to move at such super speeds that they smash together. The nuclei (the centers) of the atoms fuse together, in groups of four, forming a heavier atom called helium. The shock of the collision is so great that part of the atom is converted into energy. It is this energy that provides the light and heat for the Earth. It is this energy that causes our weather.

Heat Wave

How does heat from the Sun reach us?

You need:
a 6″ to 8″ (15-20cm) length of cord or ribbon

What to do:
Hold one end of the ribbon and shake it.

What happens:
The movement you make travels the length of the ribbon, like a wave.

Why:
Energy often moves from one place to another in waves. Short waves carry light and heat from the Sun to Earth. Longer waves carry other forms of energy.

When energy moves by waves it is called radiant energy.

Why Is Spring Sometimes Late?

Why does spring come later in some places?

You need:

an aluminum plate
an unshaded lamp
a cup of dark soil

a cup of light sand
2 room thermometers

What to do:

Place the plate beside the lamp. Fill half the plate with dark soil and half with sand. Stick thermometers into each one.

Jot down the temperature of each side. Then turn on the lamp, let the plate stand for a half hour, and compare the new temperatures with the starting ones.

What happens:

The dark soil gets hotter.

Why:

The light sand bounces back the light energy before it can change to heat energy. The dark soil soaks up the light and converts it to heat.

This is what happens when the Sun's rays reach the Earth. The dark-colored areas absorb the sunlight and heat up quickly. Light-colored areas reflect the sunlight and remain cool.

Earth does not heat up evenly. The air around dark soil becomes warmer than it does around sand or snowcapped mountains. And so, spring comes later in snow-covered countries.

Black, White, and Shiny

Here is another way to find out how different shades and surfaces affect heat.

You need:

3 tin cans
white and black paint
  (acrylic paint is fine)
cardboard or index cards
warm water
a thermometer

What to do:

Paint one can white, inside and out; paint the second black; leave third shiny.

1. Fill the three cans with warm water of the same temperature. Record the temperature.

Cover each can with an index card or cardboard, and set all three on a tray in a cool place. Record the temperature of the water in each can at five-minute intervals, for fifteen or twenty minutes.

2. Fill the cans with very cold water. Record the temperatures in each can. Then cover them and place them in a warm place or in the Sun. Record the temperature of the water in each can at five minute intervals, for fifteen or twenty minutes.

What happens:

In both cases, the black can heats up the most, the shiny can the least.

Why:

Again, the dark can absorbs best and turns the light into heat. The others reflect or give back the light before it can turn to heat.

Let It Snow

Save this one for a snowy day.

You need:
a snowstorm
a square of aluminum foil
a square of black cloth

What to do:
After a snow, put the square of black cloth and the square of aluminum foil on the snow.

Let both stay in the Sun for an hour.

Then see which has absorbed the most heat and has sunk the deepest.

What happens:
The black cloth will be deeper in the snow than the foil.

Why:
The dark cloth absorbed the light, which turned into heat—and melted the snow. The foil reflected the light before it turned into heat.

Land vs. Water

Which gets hotter—land or water?

You need:

2 plastic cups
a half-cup of water
a thermometer
a half-cup of soil
 or sand

What to do:

Place the water in one container and the soil in the other. Cool them off in the refrigerator.
 Then place both in sunlight for 15 minutes.
 Measure their temperature.

What happens:

The soil gets warm, while the water remains cool.

Why:

In sunlight, soil and sand both heat up faster than water. It's not only because land is darker than water and retains the heat. In water, the heat can go farther down and spread out. Soil keeps the heat on the surface. If you dig down on a hot beach, you find that the sand underneath is cool. Sunlight can't pass through it. The surface, therefore, becomes very hot.

 But, in addition, the specific heat of water is higher. This means it takes more heat to raise the temperature of water than it takes for the same amount of soil or sand.

 These are the reasons why, on a sunny day, land feels warmer than water.

Water vs. Air

Why is it warmer in summer and milder in winter near the ocean than inland?

You need:
a cold winter day
  (or a refrigerator)
an empty glass

a glass filled
  with water

What to do:
Put the two glasses on a cold window (or in the refrigerator) for about fifteen minutes.

What happens:
The water-filled glass feels warmer than the empty glass.

Why:
The "empty" glass is, of course, filled with air. Both air and glass lose their heat much more rapidly than the water. The glass with water does not let the cold air in and the water keeps the glass warmer longer.

That's why the world's oceans help to store up warmth from the Sun. In winter, the oceans cool off more slowly than the land, so a city near an ocean stays warmer in winter than an inland city. Oceans also warm up more slowly in summer, so a seaside city also enjoys a milder summer.

Time in the Sun

Why is summer hotter than winter? This experiment will demonstrate one reason.

You need:
a piece of black construction paper or black cloth

What to do:
Place the black paper or cloth in the Sun for one minute. Feel it. Then place the paper in the Sun for five minutes. Feel it again.

What happens:
The longer in the Sun, the hotter the paper feels.

Why:
The amount of heat increases, because it is absorbed and retained.

One reason summer is hotter than winter is that the Sun shines fifteen hours a day in July but only nine hours a day in December—since every day the Sun rises a little later and sets a little earlier. In the Southern Hemisphere, it is the reverse—the Sun shines longest in December and least in July.

Why Is Summer Hotter Than Winter?

Here's proof that the direct rays of the Sun are hotter than slanted rays.

You need:

2 tin can lids   black paint

What to do:

Paint both sides of two tin can lids with black paint and let them dry.

Prop one up so that the Sun hits it directly. Place the other flat so that the sunlight hits it at a slant.

Let both stand for ten minutes and then touch the two lids.

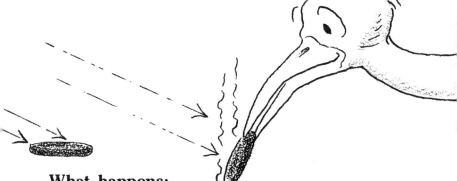

What happens:

The lid facing the Sun directly gets much hotter than the one hit at slant.

Why:

In summer the Sun's rays hit Earth more directly than in winter. That's why summer weather is hotter.

Why Is the Equator Hotter Than the North Pole?

Here's why the direct rays of the Sun are hotter than slanted rays.

You need:

a flashlight   a sheet of paper

What to do:

Shine the flashlight straight down on a sheet of paper. Then tilt the flashlight so that its rays strike the paper at a slant, as in the illustration below.

What happens:

When you point the flashlight straight down, it makes a small circle of light on the paper.

When you tilt it so that its rays strike the paper at a slant, it makes a larger, dimmer, oval shape.

Why:

Both the oval and the circle were made by the same source of light (the flashlight). Therefore, the oval has the same amount of light as the circle. Since the oval is bigger, the light in the oval must be spread more thinly.

In the same way, a slanted ray of sunlight spreads out more thinly over the Earth's surface than a ray that shines straight down. While both rays carry the same amount of heat from the Sun, the heat carried by the slanted ray is spread out and less intense.

SUN

— — slanting rays — — — —

— direct rays — — —

— — slanting rays — — — —

EARTH

So, places at and near the equator—where the Sun shines directly—get two-and-one-half times as much heat as the North and South Pole where the Sun always shines indirectly.

Shadow Thermometer

The higher the Sun is in the sky, the more direct—and the hotter—are the Sun's rays on the Earth.

A simple way to measure the position of the Sun in the sky is to measure the length of the shadows it casts.

You need:

a lamppost or fence post or flagpole or tree
a yardstick or tape measure
a notebook and a pen or pencil

What to do:

Choose a lamppost or a fence post or a young tree to cast your shadow.

Starting in the autumn, observe and measure the length of the shadow at noon every week or two.

Make a chart that records the length of the shadow, as in the illustration. Be sure to include the date.

What happens:
The shadow gets longer each time you measure it.

Why:
The higher the Sun is in the sky at noon, the shorter the shadow it casts. The lower the Sun is in the sky, the longer the shadow.

As autumn changes into winter, the Sun's path across the sky appears lower and farther south each day. Its rays strike the Earth at more and more of a slant. As a result, it heats the Earth less and less. The rays from the Sun are more direct in warmer weather and more slanted in colder weather.

Of course, if you start this experiment in the winter or spring, instead of getting longer, the shadows will gradually get shorter as the Sun rises higher in the sky and its rays strike the Earth more directly.

LENGTH VS. HEIGHT

Here is a simple way to see how the length of a shadow changes when the source of light changes position.

You need:
2 pencils   a sheet of paper
a spool of thread   a flashlight

What to do:
Stand one of the pencils in the center of the thread spool over a sheet of white paper.

Darken the room and hold the flashlight at different angles above the pencil. Record the length of each shadow.

What happens:
When the flashlight is high and right above the pencil, the shadow is short. When the light is low and at a slant, the shadow is long.

The House Is Moving!

Step outside and watch the Earth spin!

You need:

a clear evening   a chair (optional)

What to do:

On a clear evening set out a chair or lie on the ground facing south with a corner of your house to your right. Pick a star close to the edge of the wall of the house and watch it steadily.

What happens:

In a minute or two the star disappears behind the house.

Why:

Though the sky seems to move, it is really the house that is moving—as part of the Earth that is rotating on its axis.

Does the Sun Rise in the Morning?

What causes night and day?

We know that, despite what our eyes seem to tell us, the Sun does not rise in the morning and set in the evening. Here's one way to visualize what really happens.

You need:

an unshaded lamp   a ball or an orange
a darkened room   a knitting needle

What to do:

Place the unshaded lamp near the center of a darkened room. The lamp represents the Sun. Turn on the lamp.

Push the knitting needle through the center of the ball. The ball represents the Earth.

Holding the ball by the needle, turn it counterclockwise as though it were a top, and walk around the lamp.

What happens:
Different parts of the turning ball are lit and warmed by the lamp.

Why:
Obviously, the lamp was not moving—the ball was turning. And the Sun does not move up in the sky when it rises and down when it sets—it is the Earth that is turning. Part of the Earth's surface moves towards and then away from the Sun as the Earth spins towards the east on its axis.

When we are on the side of Earth that is in shadow, it is night. When we come back into sunlight, it is day.

The Earth spins around completely every twenty-four hours. Because the Earth turns, the Sun seems to "set" as we turn away from it and "rise" as we face it again.

CATCHING UP

It actually takes only 23 hours and 56 minutes for the Earth to spin around on its axis! It requires the other four minutes to return to its original place because, in addition to rotating, the Earth is also going around the Sun. (See page 32.)

Foucault's Pendulum

To show that the Earth rotates, you can repeat an experiment performed by the French physicist Jean Bernard Leon Foucault in 1851. He suspended a 200-foot (61km) pendulum from the Pantheon, a huge public building in Paris. The weight traced the path of the Earth on sand on the floor.

You can use your living room and trace the same path with a more modest pendulum. You don't need any sand.

You need:

10′ (3m) of nylon fishing line
　or thin strong wire
a ball
a knitting needle

a tack
a large index
　card
colored chalk

What to do:

Push the knitting needle into the ball and attach the ball to the length of string or wire. Suspend this "pendulum" from the ceiling so that it can swing freely.

Draw a chalk line on the index card and tack it to the floor directly under the knitting needle.

Start the pendulum swinging back and forth following the line on the index card. Note what happens after two or three hours.

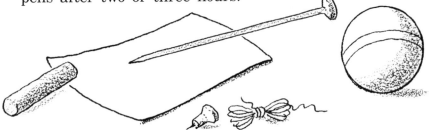

What happens:

Although the pendulum is still swinging in its original path, it is no longer swinging over the chalk mark you made.

Why:

Its inertia keeps the pendulum swinging in the same plane. But it no longer swings over the chalk mark because the room has moved! It moved because of the Earth's rotation.

A large pendulum demonstrating Earth's rotation is kept swinging in the United Nations building in New York.

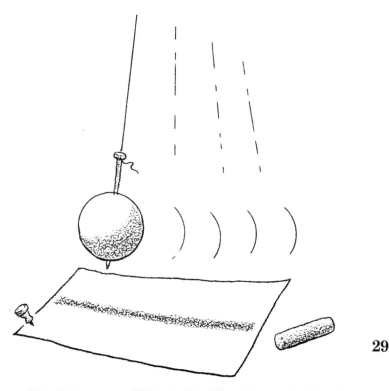

Why We See the Sun After It "Sets"

We see the Sun a couple of minutes before it comes up over the horizon at sunrise and after it has set! Here's how!

You need:
a tightly covered jar
  filled with water
books

a bare lamp bulb
  or flashlight

What to do:
Place the jar on its side on a table next to a stack of books. Put the lamp on the opposite side of the table. Stack the books so high that you can't see the light from where you are standing.

Then place the tightly covered jar filled with water in front of the stacked books, as in the illustration on page 31.

What happens:
You can see the light even though it is below the level of the top of the books.

Why:
The rounded top of the jar is like the Earth's atmosphere. It bends the rays of light and brings the image of the light into view. It creates a mirage,

such as those sometimes seen in the desert, at sea, or on hot pavement—and in the sky.

The light from the rising or setting Sun passes through a greater thickness of Earth's atmosphere than noontime sunlight does. This bends the rays of the Sun. So, at sunrise, when the Sun seems to be moving up over the horizon, we see an image of the Sun on the horizon before the Sun actually reaches it. And at sunset, because of those bending rays, we continue to see an image of the Sun briefly after the Sun actually has set.

As the World Turns

For many centuries, people believed that the Sun circled around the Earth. Now we know that not only does the Earth rotate on its axis, but it also revolves around the Sun.

You need:
a chair

What to do:
Place a chair in the middle of the room. Move around the chair.

What happens:
As you move around the chair, the chair lines up with different things in the room.

Why:
The things in the room behind the chair seem to move, though you are actually doing the moving.

In the same way, the Sun looks to us as if it is moving, but it is the Earth going around the Sun that makes it look that way.

The Earth completes its journey of 598.3 million miles (965 million km) around the Sun in a little more than 365 days, moving about 18½ miles (29.76km) per second.

It revolves around the Sun in an oval path—an ellipse. Therefore, it sometimes goes a bit faster and at other times a bit slower. The closer to the Sun, the greater the speed.

Sun in Your Room

Here's more proof that the Earth changes position in a simple experiment that will keep you busy for months!

You need:
a sunny room
a piece of chalk

a pen or pencil

What to do:
Mark a chalk line on the floor or wall where the Sun shines in your room. Keep a record of the place and the exact hour, day, and month.

A week later, at the same time of day, make another line. Again, jot down the spot and the date.

Repeat this weekly throughout the year.

What happens:
The Sun shines at a different spot in the room each week.

Why:
The movement of the Earth around the Sun causes the change in position of the line from week to week and from month to month.

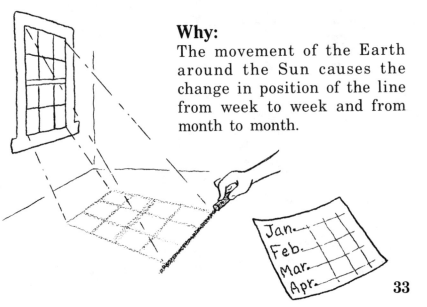

Jan.
Feb.
Mar.
Apr.

Why Do We Have Seasons?

Near the equator it remains hot all year round. At the North and South Poles it is always cold. But in most parts of the world there are four seasons every year. Why?

You need:

an orange or a rubber ball (to represent Earth)
a knitting needle or 6″ (15cm) length of wire
   (Earth's axis)
a lamp (the Sun)
a cardboard or large index card
a marker or heavy pencil

What to do:

Push the knitting needle or length of wire through the orange to represent the Earth and its imaginary axis, as in the illustration.

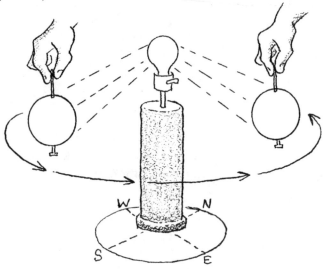

Draw an ellipse (see page 37) about 10″ in diameter (25cm) on a piece of cardboard to represent the

Earth's oval orbit. Mark the four quarter points north, south, east and west.

Place a tall, unshaded lighted lamp in the center of the cardboard to stand in for the Sun.

1. Move the orange in turn to each of the four positions holding the needle straight up and down.

Observe which part of the orange is lit up.

2. Now tilt the orange so that the axis is slanted about 23.5° away from the vertical. (See illustration).

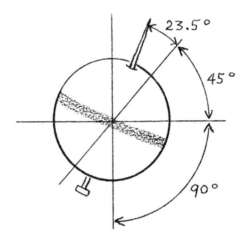

Place the orange in turn at each one of the four positions, keeping the needle tilted in the same direction.

Look at the lighted section of the orange. In each position observe which part receives the direct rays and which the slanting rays of light.

What happens:

1. When the needle is straight up and down, the same section is lit no matter where the orange is in relation to the light.

2. When the needle is at the 23.5° angle, the

amount of light depends on whether the orange is tilted towards or away from the light.

Why:

If the Earth's axis were vertical, like the orange in the first experiment, there would be no seasons.

But the axis of the Earth points to the North Star at a 23.5° slant. (See illustration.) It is this slant that makes the seasons change as the Earth revolves around the Sun.

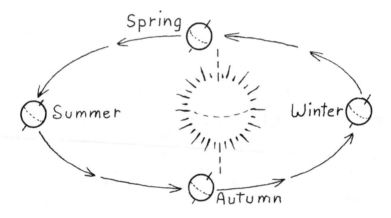

When the side we live on is tilted towards the Sun, we have summer because we receive the direct rays of the Sun. Six months later our part of the Earth is tilted away from the Sun—it is winter because we receive the Sun's rays at a slant and so get less of the Sun's heat.

At the equator, the Sun's rays are always direct. There are no seasons. At the poles, the rays always strike at a slant.

You can see, therefore, that seasons are not caused by the distance of the Earth from the Sun. Actually, in January in the Northern Hemisphere, the Earth is closer to the Sun than it is in June.

MAKING AN ELLIPSE

The Earth's path around the Sun is elliptical. Here's an easy way to make an ellipse.

Place a sheet of unlined paper on a piece of cardboard. Push two tacks (or pins) about two inches apart (5cm) into the paper. Tie the two ends of a 6″ (15cm) length of string together and loop the string around the tacks. Insert a pencil in the loop and pull the string tight. Keeping the string tight, move the pencil around and you will draw an ellipse.

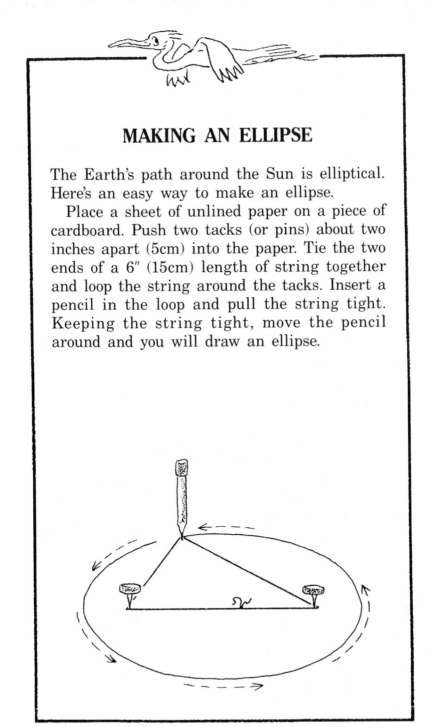

The Greenhouse Effect

All Earth is warmed by the greenhouse effect. What is it?

You need:
a clear plastic bag   2 thermometers
sunlight

What to do:
Put a thermometer into a closed, clear plastic bag and place the bag on a sunny windowsill. Place the second thermometer on the same windowsill.

After five or ten minutes, read both thermometers.

What happens:
The thermometer inside the bag reads several degrees higher than the one outside.

Why:
The Sun's rays pass through the bag easily. Once inside, however, they convert into heat, which cannot get out as easily. Therefore, the temperature inside the plastic rises. The bag warms up like a greenhouse, in which gardeners grow plants.

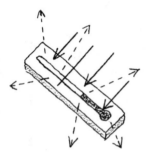 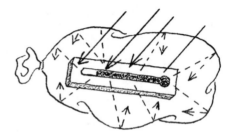

The Sun's rays pass through Earth's atmosphere in the same way. And when they convert into heat rays, they cannot get out easily. They are absorbed by the surface of the Earth, warming it as if it were a large greenhouse.

Some scientists fear that carbon dioxide in the air, from our industrial use of fuels like oil and coal, have increased the greenhouse effect. Carbon dioxide absorbs heat rays, and so they are radiated back to the Earth instead of escaping into space.

They believe that this will make the Earth warmer, causing the ice at the North and South Poles to melt. They fear sea levels will rise and flood land areas, changing our climate altogether and creating many problems.

Other scientists predict a cooling trend, and suggest that air pollution will block out more of the Sun's radiation and prevent the greenhouse effect from increasing.

WHIRLING WINDS AND GENTLE BREEZES

We live at the bottom of an ocean of air we call "the atmosphere." Most of our weather changes take place in the lower three miles (five km) of this atmosphere. And most of it is caused by the wind— as it spreads the heat of the Sun from warm areas to colder ones.

Wind is simply air that moves. But what is air? What gets it moving? Why is it sometimes so destructive?

EARTH'S WIND RECORDS

Fastest surface wind speed recorded: 231 miles an hour (370km)
Place: Mt. Washington, New Hampshire
Date: April 12, 1934

Windiest place: gale winds reach 200 miles (320km) an hour
Place: Commonwealth Bay, Antarctica

Fastest tornado winds: 286 miles (457km) an hour
Place: Wichita Falls, Texas
Date: April 2, 1958

World's worst tornado: killed 792
Place: South-central U.S.
Date: March 18, 1925

Fastest hurricane winds near a storm center: over 74 mph (118km)

Hurricane with highest wind gusts: 175-180 mph (280-288km)
Place: Central Keys and lower southwest Florida coast
Date: August 29-September 13, 1960

World's worst hurricane (unleashed floods that killed one million):
Place: Bangladesh
Date: 1970

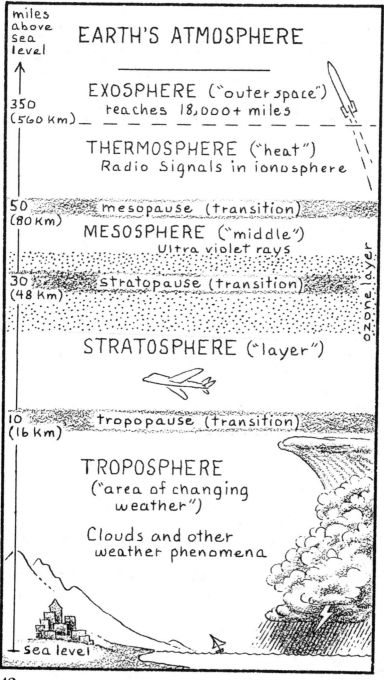

EARTH'S ATMOSPHERE

miles above sea level

EXOSPHERE ("outer space")
reaches 18,000+ miles

350 (560 km)

THERMOSPHERE ("heat")
Radio signals in ionosphere

50 (80 km)
mesopause (transition)
MESOSPHERE ("middle")
Ultra violet rays

30 (48 km)
stratopause (transition)

STRATOSPHERE ("layer")

ozone layer

10 (16 km)
tropopause (transition)

TROPOSPHERE
("area of changing weather")

Clouds and other weather phenomena

sea level

Air Takes Up Space

How do we know air is really there?

You need:

a funnel
a soda bottle
water

wide masking tape
or clay

What to do:

Put the funnel into the mouth of an empty soda bottle. Stretch the tape around the funnel and the bottle's mouth, or pack the clay around the neck of the bottle so that there is no space between the bottle and the funnel.

Pour water into the funnel.

What happens:

The water remains in the funnel. It does not flow into the bottle.

Why:

The "empty" bottle is already full of air. It takes up space and prevents the water from entering.

If you remove the masking tape, the results will be very different because the air will be able to escape!

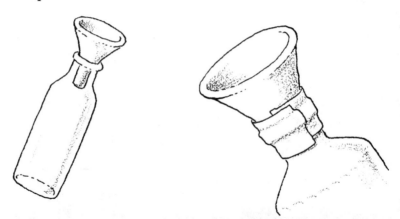

Air Has Weight

Air is a real substance. It not only takes up space, but it has weight. Here's proof.

You need:

a ruler   2 balloons   string
a hanger   tape   or thread

What to do:

Suspend the ruler from the hanger by attaching a string to the middle of it. Then tape each balloon the same distance from the ends of the ruler. Make sure that the ruler is in balance.

Now remove one of the balloons and blow it up. Tie a knot to keep it closed. Replace it at the same spot on the ruler.

What happens:

The balloon filled with air pulls the ruler down.

Why:

The balloon filled with air is heavier than the other one. Air has weight. It is actually quite heavy. At sea level air weighs 14.7 lbs. per square inch (6.6kg). On a mountaintop, air is a little thinner and weighs less.

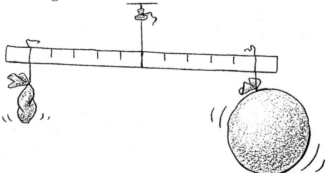

A Lot of Hot Air

Why does warm air take up more space than cold?

You need:

a balloon   a pan of hot water
a narrow-necked soda bottle

What to do:

Stretch the balloon slightly and pull it over the neck of the soda bottle.

Place the bottle in the pan of hot water and let it stand for several minutes.

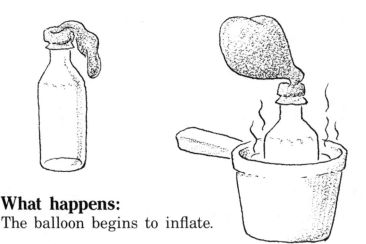

What happens:

The balloon begins to inflate.

Why:

The air in the balloon expands when it is heated. The molecules move faster and farther apart. That's what makes the balloon stretch.

And that's exactly how hot air works *outside* the balloon. Warm air is less dense than cold. It takes up more space than the same amount of cold air—and weighs less than the amount of cold air occupying the same space.

45

Air Currents and Wind

You can create an air current—and see what it does.

You need:
talcum powder
a cloth   a lamp

What to do:
Sprinkle the powder on a cloth and shake a little of it near the unlit lamp. Notice what happens.

Then light the lamp. After a few minutes, when it is hot, shake some more powder off the cloth.

What happens:
Before you turn the bulb on, the powder sinks slowly down through the air. After the bulb is hot, the powder rises.

Why:
The air, warmed by the lighted bulb, rises—carrying the talc with it. The denser, cooler air sinks.

This is what happens in nature, too. Warmer air pushes upward because it is less dense, and cooler air flows in to take its place.

Air that moves up and down (vertically) is called an air current. Wind is air that moves on the same level (horizontally).

The speed of the air currents and wind depends upon how much the temperature of one region differs from another. The direction of the wind depends on the location of these areas.

How Much Oxygen Is in the Air?

Air is a mixture of invisible, tasteless gases, including oxygen. How much oxygen is there in air?

You need:

a glass measuring cup
  or a glass jar
steel wool

a dish of water
a pencil

What to do:

Poke one end of a pencil into a clean, soapless piece of steel wool. Moisten the steel wool. Then prop up the pencil—with the steel wool on top—in a dish of water. Cover it with the measuring cup. Let it stand for two or three days.

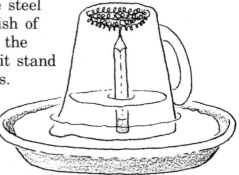

What happens:

The steel wool rusts—and the water rises until it fills about one-fifth of the jar.

Why:

The rusting process uses up the oxygen from the air in the glass, creating an area of low pressure. Water rushes into the cup to take the place of the used-up oxygen. Since oxygen makes up approximately one-fifth of the composition of air, the air rises to the height of one-fifth of the cup.

The rest of the air is mostly nitrogen, with a few traces of several other gases, including carbon dioxide.

What Causes an Air Inversion?

What happens during an air inversion? 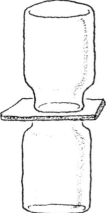 HOT

You need:

2 glass jars   cold water
hot water   a piece of twine
a safety match
a cardboard or index card

What to do:

Rinse one jar with very cold water, and the other with hot water. Dry them thoroughly.

With a cardboard between them, place the jars mouth to mouth with the warm jar on the bottom.

Light the end of the twine with a match so that it smokes. Direct the smoke into the bottom jar, as you lift the cardboard. When the smoke fills the bottom jar, pull out the cardboard.

Try the experiment with the cold jar on the bottom and the warm one on top. What happens this time?

What happens:

When the warm jar is on the bottom, the smoke rises from the lower to the upper jar. When the cold air is on bottom, the smoke is trapped and cannot rise.

Why:

The smoke rises as the warm air rises and the cold, denser air sinks. But when the warm air is trapped below the cold air, the smoke is also trapped.

This is what happens in Earth's atmosphere when a layer of warm air holds down the dust particles. This is an "air inversion." If the air is polluted, our eyes may smart, and we may cough or find it difficult to breathe.

The Air Pollution Control Laboratory records the air pollution index, which they compute based on the amount of sulphur dioxide, carbon monoxide and smoke in the air. The average daily index is 12. An emergency level is placed at 50.

Is Your Air Polluted?

You don't need complicated instruments to find out whether the air around you is dirty!

You need:

a large empty can
(the type that
held coffee or juice)

a sheet of white paper
a magnifying glass
(optional)

What to do:

Line the coffee can with the white paper. Then place it outside the window for a week or two.

Take the can in and carefully remove the paper. Examine it—with a magnifying lens if possible.

What happens:

Dust and debris discolor the paper.

Why:

Impurities pass into the air from car exhausts and smokestacks and other sources. They pollute the air and remain there if no wind blows them away—or if a layer of warm air above them acts as a blanket (see page 49). Sometimes this dust in the air causes a haze, in which it is hard to see (see page 81).

Prevailing Winds

The Earth rotates—spins—from west to east. This affects the direction in which our winds blow. Here's a simple experiment that helps to explain why some winds blow from the same direction most of the time.

You need:
a marble
a turntable (a lazy Susan or stereo turntable)

What to do:
Roll a marble from the center of the turntable to the edge. Note what happens.

Then start the turntable spinning. Aim the marble at the center to the same point on the edge.

Finally, try rolling the marble from the edge to the center.

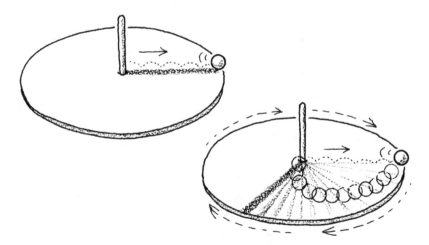

What happens:
When the turntable isn't spinning, the marble rolls in a straight line from the center to the edge.

But when the turntable is moving, the marble seems to twist as it rolls from or towards the center.

Why:
When the turntable is still, it is obvious that the marble moves in a straight line. But, even though it doesn't look that way, when the turntable moves, the marble continues to move in a straight line! The marble stops at different places on the moving turntable, and that's why it seems to twist and curve. But it reaches different places because the turntable is curving away from it. This phenomenon is known as the Coriolis effect.

In the same way, it is the spinning of the Earth on its axis that makes the winds twist and turn in certain ways.

This spin creates world-wide patterns of winds called "prevailing winds"—winds blowing from the same direction most of time. Much of world's weather depends on this great system of winds that blow in set directions.

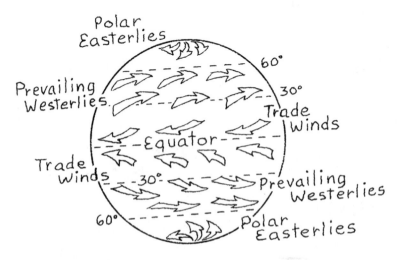

WHIRLING WINDS

Why do winds whirl counterclockwise above the equator and clockwise below?

You need:
a ball   a crayon or pencil

What to do:
Mark the top of the ball "N" for the North Pole and the bottom "S" for the South Pole.

Hold the ball so that the "N" is on top and whirl the ball from west to east. Look at the "N".

Now hold the ball high over your head and continue whirling it in the same direction.

What happens:
At the North Pole the globe is whirling counterclockwise—but the area south of the equator is whirling clockwise!

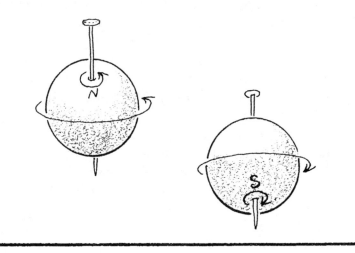

LOCAL WINDS

Some winds are occasional, brief and gentle. Other winds may last only a few minutes, but are strong enough to hurt people and property. Winds in some areas come regularly every year and last for months so that people must plan their lives around them.

Sea breezes are winds that blow from cooler high pressure areas over water to warmer low pressure areas over land.

Slope winds rush down mountain slopes into valleys or rise up from the valleys. Winds that blow down the slopes of smaller hills are called helm winds.

Foehns are warm, dry winds that occasionally blow from the mountain ridge down the side of a mountain range away from the wind (leeward side). In the Rockies, a foehn sometimes melts as much as two feet of snow overnight and is known as a *chinook*, the Indian word for snow eater. In South America, a westerly foehn blowing off the Andes is called a *zonda*, and an easterly is called a *puelche*.

A squall blows strong gusts of cold air lasting only a minute or two. It is usually accompanied by a wall of big black clouds and a short fierce shower. But a squall has been known to capsize hundreds of small boats in its brief life. Other names: williwaw in Alaska, Cockeyed Bob in Australia.

The mistrals blow cold dry air down from

the western Alps across southern France in winter, sometimes for months. The monsoons, seasonal winds in the Indian Ocean and Asia, bring torrential rains in summer. Simoons, hot, dry winds in the Sahara and Arabian Deserts, blow up suffocating clouds of sand, sometimes for a few minutes and sometimes for days.

Jet streams are fast winds that start about four miles up in the atmosphere. Caused by the sharp difference in temperature between the air in the troposphere and the stratosphere, they can be thousands of miles long and several miles wide. Sometimes they rise higher into the atmosphere and sometimes they descend towards Earth, forming storms. When they are going their way, airplane pilots like to hitch a ride on these winds.

Air Masses and Fronts

What is an air mass? A body of air thousands of miles across that has about the same temperature and amount of moisture. How does it form?

You need:
a radiator or heater   a refrigerator

What to do:
First stand in front of the radiator or heater for five to ten minutes. Then stand in front of an opened refrigerator for five to ten minutes.

What happens:
When you stand in front of the radiator or heater, you feel warm air. When you stand near the refrigerator or air conditioner, you feel cool air.

Why:
The warm radiator heats the air around it. The refrigerator cools the air around it.

Air masses work the same way. Air that lingers above a region without moving forms an air mass with the temperature and moisture of the area.

When an air mass moves on, it influences the weather of the area it passes over.

Short, hard rains

Cold air

Cold Front

When cold and warm air masses meet, they don't mix. Instead, they form a zone that is generally hundreds of miles long. That zone is called a "front." It's called a "cold front" when a cold air mass replaces a warm air mass by forcing it to rise. It's called a "warm front" when a warm air mass pushes a cold air mass ahead of it. When neither mass moves, it is called a "stationary front."

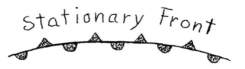

The arrival of a front indicates a change in the weather.

A cold front moves quickly. If the air is dry, it will become cloudy and the temperature will drop. If the air is moist, a cold front will bring thunderstorms and hail, but they won't last long.

A warm front moves in more slowly. If the air is dry, wispy clouds will form. But if the air is moist, the sky will become gray and the rain or snow that follows may last for days.

After the front moves on, usually there will be fair weather—warm if the warm air mass remains, cold if the cold air mass remains.

Air Pressure and Weather Predictions

Air pressure and the way it is changing helps you predict how weather will change in the next few hours and days.

You need:

a piece of broken balloon
  or other rubber scrap

a tape or string
a funnel

What to do:

Cover the wide mouth of the funnel with the piece of rubber and tape it on tightly.

Suck some air from the narrow end of the funnel and notice what happens to the rubber.

Turn the funnel upside down and suck the air in again. Then turn the funnel sideways and suck in the air.

What happens:

When you suck in the air, the rubber is pulled in, whatever the direction of the funnel.

Why:

When you suck in the air, you are removing it from the inside of the funnel. When you do that, the push of air outside the funnel is greater than the push of the air from inside, even when you hold the funnel upside down or sideways. Air pushes— presses—equally in all directions.

You already know that the air over each square inch of the Earth's surface, pulled by the Earth's gravity, weighs 14.7 lbs (6.6 kg). This weight is known as air pressure.

When cool, dense air presses down on the Earth, the air pressure is usually high. Warm, less dense air rises away from the Earth, and so, when it's warm, we generally have low air pressure.

High pressure usually brings clear weather, while low pressure brings bad weather and strong winds. Changing pressure also brings winds.

When there are big differences in air pressure, air rushes out of the high pressure area to fill the low pressure area. Then there are strong, sometimes savage winds. If the difference in pressure is small, air gently drifts towards the low pressure area and we have gentle breezes.

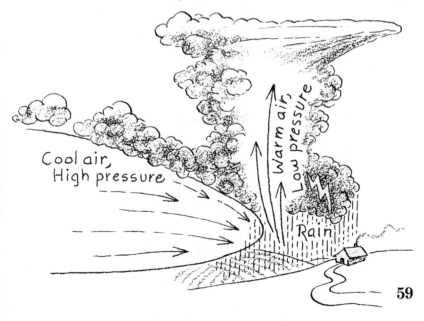

Cool air,
High pressure

Warm air,
Low pressure

Rain

A Trick Can

Just for fun! This one is better to do over a sink or a basin.

You need:

an empty can with
    a screw top (a floor wax
    can, for instance)

a hammer
a nail
water

What to do:

Using the hammer and nail, punch a small hole near the bottom of the empty can. Fill the can with water and cap it quickly. Then remove the top.

What happens:

The water does not flow out from the hole—until you remove the top.

Why:

Air is pressing up harder than the water is pressing down—until you remove the top of the can. Then the air pressing down on the opening in the can, added to the pressure of the water, makes the downward pressure greater than the upward pressure.

BALLOT'S LAW

Using Ballot's Law we can find the location of high and low pressure areas.

Buys Ballot, a Dutch scientist, discovered in 1857 that there was a relationship between the direction of the wind and the location of the high pressure and low pressure areas that were causing it.

In the Northern Hemisphere, if you stand with your back to the wind, the high pressure area will be on your right and the low pressure on your left. In the Southern Hemisphere, it is exactly the opposite.

A change in wind often brings a change in weather. In the Northern Hemisphere a south or west wind brings warm or mild, wet weather. A north or east wind brings colder, drier weather, especially in winter. All winds are named after the direction from which they are blowing.

Tornado!

Though most of the destruction done by tornadoes is caused by the terrible speed of the whirling winds, lowered air pressure may also cause a great deal of damage.

You need:
a plastic bottle or jar

What to do:
Remove the air from inside the bottle by sucking on it.

What happens:
The bottle collapses.

Why:
The air around the outside of the bottle pushes inward because you've removed some of the inside air. Normally, the air inside the bottle would balance the outer force.

The pressure inside the bottle drops, just as it does in the center of a tornado.

A tornado starts when cold dry air coming from the west catches up with unusually warm, moist air from the south. The result is a whirling wind with thick, black clouds and thunderstorms. Water vapor is swept upward as gusts of warm air rise in a spiraling motion. When the air cools, it forms the tornado's twisting, funnel-shaped cloud.

The funnel-shaped wind cloud whirls at enormous speeds and picks up dust, trees, animals, water, automobiles, houses—anything in its path—and whirls them upward. The rapidly rising column of air within the funnel lowers the pressure in the funnel's center as the tornado advances.

A house can be crushed in the midst of a tornado just as the bottle was crushed—because the air pressure in the center of the tornado is lower than the normal pressure inside the house.

The tornado spins, smashing and destroying, until all the heated air that was near land has been squeezed up by the cooler, heavier, inflowing air. Then the air stops flowing and the tornado dies.

Bernoulli's Law

The air pressure of a tornado is so low that houses in its path may be destroyed. What causes this low air pressure?

You need:
2 apples
2 strings about 12″ to 16″ long (30 to 40cm)

What to do:
Hang the apples a few inches apart (about 5-7cm). Blow hard between them.

What happens:
Instead of being pushed apart, the apples move towards each other.

Why:
By blowing between the apples, you cause the air between the apples to move. This lessens the air pressure between them. Then the air on the sides of the apples pushes them towards the area of lower pressure.

As the speed of air increases, the pressure of the air decreases. The faster air moves, the less pressure it has. This was discovered in 1738 by the Swiss physicist, Daniel Bernoulli.

This lessening of pressure caused by high-speed air movement is one of the reasons a tornado is so destructive. Objects are propelled into whirling air by the stronger pressure of air around them.

MORE ABOUT TORNADOES

A tornado seldom lasts more than an hour and usually covers about two city blocks—less than one-tenth of a mile (158m). Only two per cent of tornadoes are classified as "violent." They may last longer, with winds of up to 300 miles (480km) an hour, and may cover a path of up to 26 miles (42km) long and a mile wide (1.6km). They can be the most destructive storms on Earth. Most tornado injuries and deaths result from flying objects whirled about by the wind.

Tornadoes are sometimes called cyclones and twisters.

Eye of a Hurricane

A hurricane is a violent storm that starts in tropical waters. In the middle of the swirling winds of a hurricane is the calm "eye."

You need:
a yo-yo or a button
   on a string

What to do:
Whirl the yo-yo
around your head.

What happens:
The yo-yo seems to try to pull away from the hand holding its string. The faster you whirl it, the stronger the pull is.

Why:
The explanation is centrifugal force, the force that pulls an object outward when moving in a circle.

In the same way, the winds of a hurricane tend to pull away from the center as their speed increases. When the winds move fast enough, a hole develops in the center—the mark of a full-fledged hurricane.

The eye of a hurricane is a cloudless hole, usually about ten miles wide, within which all is calm and peaceful. But surrounding the eye, howling winds swirl at speeds up to 150 miles an hour, with gusts up to 180 miles (288km) an hour.

Hurricane winds may cover an area up to sixty miles wide. They may rage for a week or more, and travel tens of thousands of miles over sea and land.

Hurricanes arise when warm moist air over tropical waters rises above 6,000 feet (1800m). The water vapor condenses (turns to raindrops) releasing heat energy. This in turn forces columns of air to rise up quickly (updrafts) to heights of 50,000 to 60,000 feet (180,000m) and fluffy, cauliflower-like cumulus clouds become towering thunderheads. (See illustration.)

Then air from outside the storm area moves in to replace the rising air. It begins to swirl around the updraft because of the Earth's spin. As it swirls over the surface of the sea, it soaks up more and more water vapor, which then gets pulled into the updraft, releasing still more energy as more of the water vapor condenses. The updraft then rises faster, pulling in larger amounts of air and water vapor from the edge of the storm, and the air swirls even faster around the "eye."

Hurricane winds circulate counterclockwise in the Northern Hemisphere and clockwise in the Southern Hemisphere.

They are called cyclones in the Indian Ocean, typhoons in the Pacific, and willy-willies in Australia.

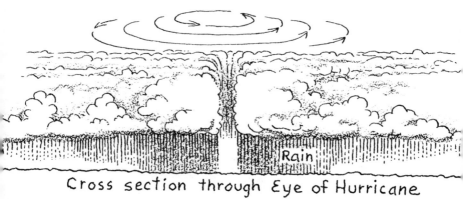

Cross section through Eye of Hurricane

WATER, WATER, EVERYWHERE

How does water get into the air? Why does it come out of the air? Why does it snow? When does it rain? sleet? hail?

EARTH'S PRECIPITATION RECORDS

Greatest rainfall in one day: 73.62 inches (184cm)
Place: Le Reunion, island in Indian Ocean
Date: March 15, 1952

Greatest rainfall in one month: 366 inches (915cm)
Place: Assam, India
Date: July, 1961

Greatest rainfall in one year: 1,041 inches (2,602cm)
Place: Assam, India
Date: August, 1880, to August, 1881

Highest average annual rainfall: 460 inches (1,150cm)
Place: Mount Waialeale, Kauai, Hawaii

Highest number of thunderstorms: 322 days a year
Place: The island of Java, Indonesia

Lowest annual rainfall: 0.03 inches (0.08cm)
Place: Arica, Chile

Longest period without rain: 400 years
Place: desert of Atacama, Chile

Greatest snowfall in one day: 75.8 inches (189.5cm)
Place: Silver Lake, Colorado
Date: April 14-15, 1921

Greatest snowfall in a single storm: 189 inches (472.5cm)
Place: Mt. Shasta, California
Date: Feb. 13-19, 1959

69

Water Going into the Air

Moisture in the air—humidity—is one part of a great water cycle. The main supply comes from the Earth's five oceans and from many smaller bodies of water. How does the water get into the air?

You need:
2 jars (one with a cover)   water

What to do:
Place an equal amount of water in two jars. Cover one of them. Place both on the table overnight. Check them in the morning.

What happens:
There is less water in the open jar than in the capped jar.

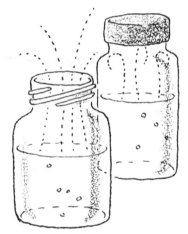

Why:
Even at room temperature, the tiny particles or molecules of water in the uncapped jar move fast enough to fly out and escape into the air. The water turns into water vapor, an invisible gas. This process is known as "evaporation."

If you've ever wondered what happens to puddles when the rain stops, that is the explanation. And that is how water gets back into the air.

Evaporation Race #1

Which container of water will evaporate faster—the flat disk or the deep jar?

You need:

a large flat dish
water
a deep narrow jar

What to do:

Place an equal amount of water in the dish and the jar. Place both, uncovered, on the table to stand overnight. Check them in the morning.

What happens:

Less water remains in the flat dish than in the narrow jar.

Why:

The molecules of water can escape only from the surface. So water will evaporate faster when the surface is large.

A wide shallow puddle, therefore, will dry up more quickly than a deep narrow one.

Wind and Water

What effect does wind have on the water in the air? Why does fanning a washed blackboard make it dry more quickly?

You need:
a line   two wet handkerchiefs
a cardboard

What to do:
Hang the two handkerchiefs to dry. Fan one with a cardboard.

What happens:
The handkerchief that is fanned dries first.

Why:
Fanning speeds up evaporation by replacing the moist air near the handkerchief with drier air. Blowing winds do the same thing with clouds in the sky.

Evaporation Race #2

What role does the Sun play in the evaporation of water in the air?

You need:
two dishes   water
a sunny window

What to do:
Half fill the two dishes with water. Place one in the Sun or on the radiator, and the other in the shade.

What happens:
The dish in the Sun dries first.

Why:
The warmer the water, the faster the molecules move into the air and the faster they evaporate.

Most water vapor comes from lakes, rivers, oceans, leaves of plants and wet ground. The heat from the Sun causes the water to change from liquid to gas, which goes into the air. As its temperature increases, air can hold more and more water. As it gets colder, it holds less and less.

Evaporation Cools Air

Liquids require heat to evaporate—and so, any place where evaporation takes place becomes cooler.

You need:

a thermometer
cotton
a rubber band

water
an eye dropper or straw

What to do:

Place the thermometer where wind will strike it. Note the temperature after a half hour or so.

Dampen a small piece of cotton and wrap it around the bulb of the thermometer. Leave it in the wind for half an hour, and again note the temperature.

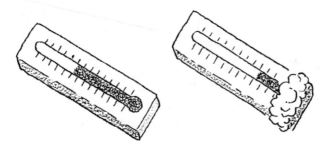

What happens:

The temperature of the thermometer with the wet cotton on it is several degrees lower than it was before.

Why:

In the process of evaporation, energy in the form of heat is removed from the thermometer. The hygrometer, one of the most important weather instruments, is based on this fact (see page 111).

Water Coming Out of the Air

We found out how water gets into the air. Let's look at how it gets out again.

You need:

an empty tin can   water
ice   vegetable dye or tea

What to do:

Remove the label from the can and fill it with ice. Add water and a few drops of vegetable dye. Let it stand on the table for a few minutes.

What happens:

The can seems to be "sweating." Drops of water form on the outside.

Why:

The drops are not colored, so they couldn't be coming from the ice water leaking out of the can. The water must come from the air.

Water vapor—water in the form of gas—in the air around the can has been cooled by the ice.

Air molecules slow down when they become cold. They move closer together and change into liquid form. This is known as "condensation."

Great amounts of water are always evaporating into the air as the Sun warms the Earth's oceans, rivers and lakes. As much as five per cent of the air can be water vapor on a day when humidity is high. The water vapor becomes part of the warmer air near the Earth's surface. Because it is less dense than cold air, this warmer air tends to rise. It rises to colder and colder levels. When it reaches a cold enough level, the water vapor changes into droplets of water. Cold air can't hold as much water vapor as warm air.

Large numbers of these little drops of water collect on dust particles as the air cools. This forms clouds. The drops fall to Earth as rain or snow, when they become too heavy to be held up by the pressure of air.

The movement of water through evaporation and condensation is called the water cycle.

Indoor Cloud

You form a cloud in your kitchen every time you boil water in a teakettle!

You need:
a teakettle of boiling water
an aluminum pie plate

What to do:
Heat water in a teakettle.
When it starts to boil,
hold the pie plate in the steam.

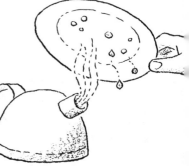

What happens:
When the water boils, a whitish "cloud" forms above the spout. When you hold the pie plate in the "cloud," drops of water form on it.

Why:
The clouds in the sky form in the same way. Heated air containing invisible water vapor rises. As it rises, it cools. The water vapor condenses into millions of tiny water droplets, forming a cloud.

On a sunny, summer day, the Sun heats up the ground quickly. The ground heats the air next to it. Because warm air is less dense than cold air, it rises. As it moves away from the hot ground, it cools. When it rises high enough and becomes cool enough, the water vapor in the air condenses—turns into water droplets. Millions of these droplets together make up one of the fluffy clouds we see in the sky. These fluffy clouds are known as cumulus clouds.

WHY CLOUDS LOOK WHITE

The white light of the Sun is really a mixture of all the colors. When sunlight enters a droplet of water, it is broken up into the different wavelengths that we see as red, orange, yellow, green, blue, indigo, and violet. Some of the colored light is reflected from the far side of the droplet back and out of the droplet.

The blue color of the sky results from the way tiny particles of dust and vapor in the air scatter light rays. The rays of shorter wavelengths (the blues and violets) are spread out more widely than the rays of longer wavelengths (the reds and yellows).

Too much dust, especially in large particles, causes the scattering of many rays—not only the blue ones. Then the sky becomes whitish or hazy. When a cloud forms, there isn't much difference in the scattering of the different wavelengths of sunlight. We see the mixture of all the colors of the spectrum and the clouds look white to us.

The sky appears red at sunset and sunrise when the longer wavelengths (the reds and yellows) are scattered more effectively. This happens because the Sun is closer to the horizon, and so its light shines at an angle closer to the surface and through more atmosphere, dust, and water droplets.

Be a Rain Maker!   HOT!

Make rain in your kitchen!

You need:
a double-boiler (or one large and one small pot
   and a small can)
water   ice cubes

What to do:
If you don't have a double-boiler, you can make your
own by stacking a small pot on top of a small can
in a slightly larger pot. Boil water in the bottom
section. Then place cold water and ice cubes
in the upper pot, and place the pot over
the boiling water.

What happens:
You see—rain!

Why:
The cold surfaces of the upper pot cool the steam
from the boiling water. The steam changes back
into water, collecting in drops. As the drops get
bigger and heavier, it "rains."

The boiling water is like the water heated by the
Sun. The steam is like the water that evaporates
into the air as water vapor. As the vapor rises, it
cools. You see clouds when droplets form. As these
droplets collect more moisture, they become heavy
enough to fall to earth as rain.

MEASURING THE SIZE OF A RAINDROP

Place a piece of cardboard on your window when it first starts to rain, and you will be able to see the size of a raindrop.

Raindrops may measure from $\frac{1}{100}$ of an inch across to $\frac{1}{4}''$ (0.25 to 1cm) across. Each is made up of millions of droplets of water.

Small raindrops—less than $\frac{2}{100}''$ across (0.5mm)—often take an hour or more to reach the ground. Light rain like this is known as drizzle. It usually falls from a layered cloud less than 1.2 miles thick (2km).

A heavy, sudden shower of large raindrops or hail falls from a heaped cumulo-nimbus cloud that might be nine miles (15km) or more deep. (See page 121.)

What Causes Smog? HOT

Smog is a combination of fog—tiny droplets of water in the air—and smoke from pollutants in the air. Let's see how it happens.

You need:
a large narrow-mouthed jar   a lighted match

What to do:
Blow hard into a large narrow-mouthed jar and then remove your lips quickly. Light a match and blow it out. While it is still smoking, dip it into the jar so that smoke enters. Blow into the jar again and again remove your lips quickly.

What happens:
Smog builds up in the jar.

Why:
When you stopped blowing the first time, the sudden lessening of pressure produced a cooling effect. This caused a small amount of water vapor to condense—turn back into droplets of water in the jar. When you added the smoke of the match, the droplets combined with tiny particles of dust from the smoke to form smog.

On dry windy days, smoke and soot from factory chimneys and automobile exhaust systems are carried high into the air and blown away. But on cool damp days with no wind, the particles hang low in the moist air to form smog.

OZONE

Ozone, the main ingredient of smog, is an oxygen with three atoms. It forms when chemicals (such as hydrocarbons and nitrogen compounds)—released by factories and machines—react to heat and sunlight.

Ozone in the lower atmosphere can make people sick. When the air quality index for ozone climbs to over 200, people are advised to stay indoors, if possible.

In the stratosphere, from ten to thirty miles (16–50km) above the Earth, a layer of ozone forms naturally, shielding Earth from the Sun's harmful ultraviolet rays. But there is now evidence of an ozone hole above Antarctica. It has been traced to the use of carbofluorides and similar compounds. These are used in refrigerators and air conditioners; in cleaning electronic equipment; in the manufacture of plastic foam; and in pressurized spray cans. If the ozone layer continues to get holes in it—or the hole that exists gets larger—scientists warn that we can expect an increase in diseases that result from the Sun's ultraviolet rays, such as skin cancer.

Refrigerator Weather

Raid your refrigerator and learn the difference between snow and sleet. If your refrigerator defrosts automatically, wait for a snowy day and collect your specimens outdoors.

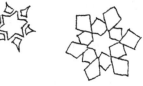

You need:
white frost (from the freezer)
   or snow (from the ground)
an ice cube
a magnifying glass

black construction
   paper or cloth
a large spoon

What to do:
Place the frost (or snow) on a piece of black paper or cloth and examine it with a magnifying glass.

Chip off a small piece of the ice cube with a large spoon and place the sliver of ice on the black cloth. Examine it under the magnifying glass.

What happens:
In the frost (or snow) you see a six-pointed star-shaped crystal. In the ice, you don't.

Why:
The frost in the refrigerator and the snowflakes in the sky form in the same way. Water vapor in the clouds—and water vapor in the refrigerator—cools down so much that instead of turning into water, it freezes into snowflakes and frost.

The ice cube forms in the same way as sleet. Both start out as water—and later freeze. Sleet starts as raindrops. When it falls through very cold air, it freezes into little bits of ice.

Dissecting a Hailstone

If you've ever been in a hailstorm, you may know how violent they can be. A hailstone was found in Ohio in 1981 that weighed thirty pounds! What causes hail?

Like sleet, hail is made from raindrops that later freeze but its formation is more involved.

You need:
a hailstone
a hammer

a sheet of newspaper

What to do:
Split open the hailstone on a newspaper. Count the number of rings you see.

What happens:
You learn how many trips up in the cold air the hailstone made before it fell to Earth.

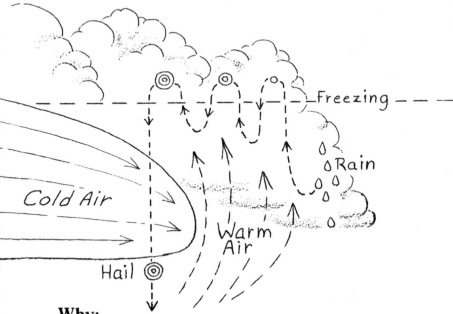

Why:
Strong winds pick up raindrops and fling them high up where the air is cold enough to freeze them into ice drops. If they fell to Earth at this point, they would be sleet. But instead of letting them fall all the way down, the winds blow them up again. In the very cold upper air, a new layer of ice freezes around the old. The ice drops fall and are blown up again and again. Finally when they are too heavy for the up-blowing wind, they clatter to the ground as hail.

Hailstones sometimes get bigger than golf balls and they have been known to do damage to crops or buildings. The largest hailstone on record measured 17.5" (44cm) and fell on Coffeyville, Kansas, on September 3rd, 1979.

What Is Lightning?

Make your own lightning! Not to worry—home-made lightning isn't dangerous. You've probably made it many times without realizing it.

You need:
a comb   a piece of wool or fur
metal doorknob

What to do:
Rub the comb with a piece of wool or fur. Hold it near a metal doorknob.

What happens:
You produce
a small spark.

Why:
By rubbing the comb, you charge it with electricity. The spark is made when the charge jumps to the uncharged (neutral) doorknob. The spark is the passage of an electrical charge between two objects.

You may have seen a similar spark when you walked over a rug and then touched a doorknob. You may have heard a crackling sound while combing your hair or petting a cat. These are all examples of static electricity.

Lightning is a huge electric spark that results when charges jump from one cloud to another or to the ground. Though lightning may discharge an enormous amount of electricity, it lasts much too brief a time to be trapped into useful energy.

On a hot humid summer day, when hot air climbs quickly, moisture in the air condenses to form billions of water drops and ice crystals. These pick up tiny electric charges as they move through the air. The violent air currents in thunderclouds move different-sized drops and dust particles at different speeds. Those of the same size and with similar amounts of electricity get concentrated in the same part of the cloud. A very high positive electrical charge is often formed in the cold higher parts, while near the ground the thundercloud usually is negatively charged.

The big difference between the charges at the top and the bottom of the cloud creates a powerful voltage or electric pressure. This "push" sends a flash of lightning streaking through the cloud between those parts with opposite electric charges.

DOES LIGHTNING EVER STRIKE TWICE IN THE SAME SPOT?

Despite sayings to the contrary, lightning may hit the same place or the same person several times. The United States Weather Bureau reports the case of a National Park Ranger who was hit seven times!

STORM WARNINGS

A summer thunderstorm clears the air and leaves us refreshed. The rumble and roar of thunder is all noise and no bite, and by the time you hear it, all danger is usually past. But flashes of lightning may be dangerous. They can start fires, knock over trees, injure or even kill people.

Lightning takes the shortest path. It hits the highest objects—a tall tree or house, a tower, a person standing alone in a flat field. Modern skyscrapers, however, are built so that lightning may strike them without doing any harm.

Here's what the weather service says to do, if a storm is close.

If You're Outdoors:
Go indoors, if possible—inside a house or large building. If you can't do that, get into an automobile. (Not a convertible!) Don't take refuge in a shed—metal or wood.

Don't stand next to a telephone pole. Keep away from a lone tree. Don't stand on a hilltop. Avoid being the tallest object. Seek shelter in low areas under small trees. If you're in a field, crouch on your knees and bend over.

Keep away from metal pipes, rails, metal fences, and wire clotheslines. Don't carry anything made of metal. Don't ride a bicycle or a scooter. If you're in a group, spread out. Keep several yards apart.

Keep away from water. If you are swimming, get out. Don't stay out in a boat or stand under a beach umbrella.

If You're Inside:

Keep away from windows and doors. Stay away from water taps, sinks, tubs, the stove—anything that could conduct electricity. Don't use electric appliances—the TV, irons, toasters, mixers.

Don't use the telephone unless there's an emergency.

What Causes Thunder?

You hear a crackle when you raise a spark. What causes that sound and what causes the roar of thunder?

You need:
a balloon or a paper bag

What to do:
Blow up the paper bag or the balloon. Tie it with a rubber band or a piece of string.

Then place one hand on the top and one hand on the bottom of the bag and pop it.

What happens:
You get a small clap of thunder.

Why:
You created thunder by causing a small quantity of air to move fast. An object produces sound when it vibrates—moves back and forth or up and down. Humans only hear sound when an object vibrates at least sixteen times a second—and not more than 20,000 times a second.

When a flash of lightning passes through the atmosphere, it heats the nearby air, and causes it to expand rapidly. It is this movement that causes the sound. A short crash of thunder results from a short flash of lightning. Rolling thunder occurs when lightning covers a large area, or when clouds, mountains or other obstructions cause echoes.

HOW FAR AWAY IS THE STORM?

When you see a flash of lightning, start counting seconds like this: "and one and, and two and, and three and"—and continue until you hear a roar of thunder. Divide the number you get by 5 (for miles) or by 3 (for kilometers). That will give you a rough estimate of how far away the center of the storm is.

Why:
Lightning and thunder take place at the same time, but light and sound travel to us at different speeds, and so reach us at different times. Light travels at 186,000 miles per second (300,000km) and takes only a fraction of a second to reach us. We see lightning the moment it flashes.

It takes about 5 seconds for sound to travel a mile (3 seconds for a kilometer).

When a thunderstorm is near, the thunderclap sound is loud and sharp. When it is far away, it is a low rumble. Ordinarily, you can't hear thunder more than 10 or 15 miles (16–24km) away. If you see lightning and hear thunder at just about the same moment, the storm is right above you.

Make Your Own Rainbow

After the storm comes the rainbow. Here's one you can have any time.

You need:
a glass of water   a sheet of white paper
a sunny window

What to do:
Stand a glass of water on a window ledge in bright sunlight. Place the sheet of paper on the floor.

What happens:
You see the colors of the rainbow.

Why:
You are separating the various colors (the spectrum) that make up white light. When light passes at a slant from the air through the glass of water, the rays change direction—they are "refracted." Each color bends differently: violet bends the most and red the least. So, when the light comes out of

the glass of water, the different colors travel in slightly different directions and strike the sheet of paper at different places.

It is the same with a rainbow in the sky. It is simply a curved spectrum, made when sunlight shines through water drops in the air at an angle of between 40° and 42° with the horizon. The water drops bend the Sun's rays.

The Sun has to be behind you if you're going to see a rainbow in the sky. So you'll only see a rainbow early in the morning, when the Sun is shining in the east and showers are falling in the west—or in the late afternoon, when the Sun is shining in the west and showers are falling in the east.

The arc you see from the ground is just a part of the rainbow. Only if you happen to be flying in a plane will you see a rainbow's full circle.

BUILDING A
WEATHER STATION

With everyday materials, you can make the instruments you need to keep track of temperature, air pressure, wind direction and wind speed, humidity and rainfall.

Don't feel too bad if your predictions are not always accurate. Weathermen are not always right, either—even with the help of weather satellites circling the Earth, radar, balloon-borne instruments, and super-speed computers to help their surface observations!

KEEPING RECORDS

Weather maps are based on information collected by hundreds of local weather stations.

You may want to check the daily findings of your "station" with your local radio and television meteorologists—and with the information published in your local paper.

You can keep records and report your findings in several ways.

When you measure the various weather factors, using instruments and observations, make a chart of your findings, such as the one on page 94.

You may also want to make a station model. It's a handy way to show the same information. It uses a system of symbols that can easily fit on a map. You can adapt the symbols below so that you can record and compare your daily findings. This sample model is reporting a partly cloudy day, northwest winds at 20 miles (32km) an hour, temperature of 65°F (18.3°C), and a dew point of 50°F (10°C). Air pressure is reported in millibars (see pg. 99). You can substitute H (for high) and L (for low), and + for rising and − for falling pressure.

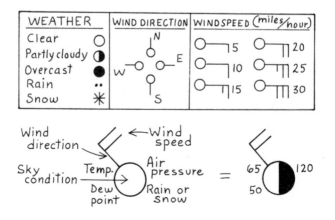

Straw Thermometer

How does a thermometer work? Make your own and find out.

You need:

a medicine bottle
  or small jar
a cork to fit
a few drops of food
  coloring

a felt-tipped pen
a glass straw
  or medicine dropper tube
a nail
water

What to do:

Dig out a hole in the cork with the nail and fit the straw or tube through it.

Fill the bottle to the brim with water colored with a drop or two of food coloring and cap it securely. Mark the line the water rises to in the tube with a felt-tipped pen.

Note the height of the water in the straw at room temperature, and also at different times and places—on a sunny windowsill, in the refrigerator, in a pot of hot water.

What happens:

The water goes up the tube when the temperature is warm and goes down when it is cold.

Why:

We measure temperature by the changes made. Temperature is really a measure of whether one object absorbs heat from or loses heat to another object.

Liquids expand when heated and contract when cooled. The liquid of the thermometer absorbs heat. It expands when it contacts anything warmer than itself, and contracts when contacting something cooler. Mercury and colored alcohol are usually used as the liquid in thermometers because they react so quickly.

Makers of commercial weather thermometers use a sealed glass tube that has a little bulb blown out at one end. They mark the thermometer's scale by placing its bulb in contact with melting ice. The point at which the liquid contracts is 32° for a Fahrenheit scale and 0° for a Centigrade scale. Then the bulb is placed in the steam from boiling water. The point at which it expands is marked 212°F or 100°C.

You can make a scale for your straw thermometer by comparing its levels with a commercial weather thermometer.

Gabriel Fahrenheit, a German physicist, devised the first commonly used scale in 1714. About thirty years later, a Swedish astronomer, Anders Celsius, established the centigrade scale, also known as the celsius scale.

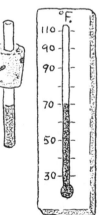

The first thermometer was invented in 1593 by the Italian physicist Galileo.

Temperature Conversion

°FAHRENHEIT		°CENTIGRADE
212	*water boils*	100
194	—	90
176	—	80
158	—	70
140	—	60
136	*highest Earth temperature ever recorded*	57.7
122	—	50
104	—	40
98.6	*body temperature*	37
86	—	30
68	—	20
50	—	10
32	*water freezes*	0
14	—	−10
−4	—	−20
−22	—	−30
−40	—	−40
−58	—	−50
−76	—	−60
−94	—	−70
−112	—	−80
−129	*coldest Earth temperature ever recorded*	−89
−130	—	−90

To convert from F° to C°: Subtract 32° and then multiply by 5. Divide the result by 9.
  For a quick estimate of Centigrade:
  Deduct 30 and divide by 2.

To convert from C° to F°: Multiply by 9. Divide the result by 5. Then add 32.
  For a quick estimate of Fahrenheit:
  Multiply by 2 and add 30.

READING A BAROMETER

At sea level, in normal weather, the mercury in a barometer measures 29.92 inches (1013.2 millibars). In cool, dry weather the mercury level rises. In warm, wet weather, it drops, just the way the water does in the bottle barometer.

The Weather Bureau prefers the mercury barometer to the aneroid (a barometer made without liquid) because it is more accurate. The Bureau finds it more convenient to measure air pressure in millibars. Millibar readings are shortened on weather maps by dropping the first two numbers and the decimal, so that normal pressure—1013.2—for instance, is reported as 132.

The lowest barometric pressure ever recorded was 25.59 inches (870mb) on October 12, 1979, some 300 miles west of Guam in the Pacific Ocean, during a typhoon. The highest barometric pressure recorded was 32 inches (1083.8mb) in Agata, Siberia, USSR, on December 31, 1968.

Air pressure is usually lower on stormy days than on clear, dry days. So, when air pressure falls, it often indicates that a storm is approaching. A change in pressure of one tenth of an inch or more (2.5mm) in six hours means a fast change in the weather.

To change inches to millibars, multiply the number of inches by 33.87.

Bottle Barometer

You already know that the layer of air surrounding the Earth exerts a pressure of more than fourteen pounds on every square inch.

An Italian physicist named Evangelista Torricelli first figured out a way to measure this atmospheric pressure over 300 years ago. He balanced a column of mercury with a column of air. You can make a barometer that works like his with ordinary tap water.

You need:
a saucer	a plastic soda bottle
water	an index card

What to do:
Fill the saucer halfway with water. Pour water into the bottle until it is about ¾ full. Keeping your thumb on the mouth of the bottle, turn the bottle upside down. Then remove your thumb and quickly put the mouth of the bottle into the saucer of water. Paste a strip of the index card on the outside of the bottle. (See illustration.)

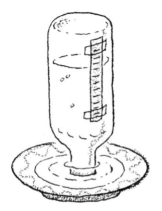

What happens:

The water doesn't pour out of the bottle. Instead, the water level drops slightly and comes to rest. Then, it moves up or down as the air pressure changes.

Why:

Air pressing against the water prevents the water from running out. The water stops moving downward when the water pressure is balanced by the pressure of the atmosphere.

Mark the index card at the point where the water settles, and you will be able to chart whether the water goes up or down in the bottle. An increase in air pressure sends the water up. A decrease drops it down. When the water in the bottle drops down, you can expect warmer, wetter weather.

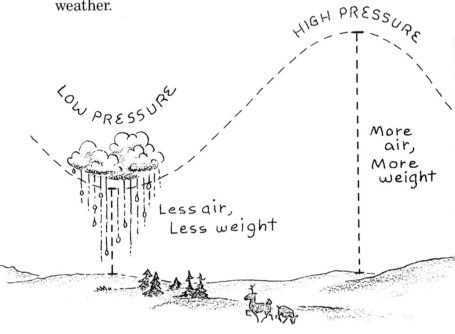

Balloon Barometer

This crude barometer also will show when there is a change in air pressure.

You need:

a drinking straw

a rubber band or piece of string

a pencil or felt-tipped pen

a piece of cardboard

a balloon or other rubber scrap

a narrow-mouthed jar

glue

What to do:

Stretch the balloon, or any odd scrap of thin rubber, such as from a torn bathing cap, over the top of the jar. Fasten it with a rubber band or string. Then glue the straw horizontally, starting from the center of the rubber, so that it extends beyond the edge of the top of the jar, as in the illustration. Attach a pin to the free end of the straw.

Prop up a marked index card so that you can follow the movement of the straw.

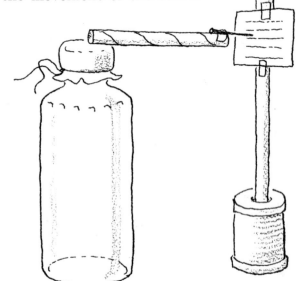

What happens:

The unattached end of the straw (the pointer) sometimes moves up and sometimes moves down.

Why:

When air pressure increases, the pressure inside the bottle is less than that of the outside air. Therefore the balloon rubber pushes down, and the pointer end of the straw moves up. When the air pressure goes down, the air inside the bottle presses harder than the outside air. The rubber pushes up and tightens, and the pointer moves down.

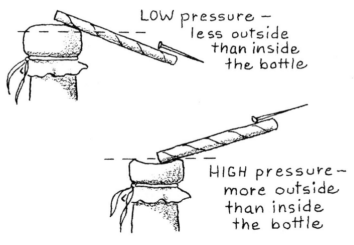

LOW pressure — less outside than inside the bottle

HIGH pressure — more outside than inside the bottle

When your pointer moves down, bad weather is probably on the way. Air pressure usually falls when a storm is approaching. When air pressure rises, it is usually a sign that the weather is going to improve.

Your balloon barometer functions a lot like the aneroid barometer. A flexible top pushes in and out as air pressure changes, and moves the pointer around a scale on the face of the instrument.

Weather Vane

If we know the direction the wind is blowing, we can sometimes locate a low pressure system and forecast the bad weather that usually comes with it. A weather vane shows wind direction.

You need:

a drinking straw

a pencil with an eraser

an old flowerpot

a red marker or crayon

a compass

an index card or piece
  of light cardboard

a pin

glue

thin wire or paper clips

What to do:

Make a one-inch (2.5cm) vertical slit in one end of a drinking straw. Using an index card or other piece of cardboard, cut out an arrow tail and glue it into the cut end of the straw, as in the illustration. Mark the other end of the straw with the red marker or crayon. Insert the straight pin through the straw about two inches (5cm) from the arrow. Push the pin into the eraser end of the pencil. Be sure the straw can move freely.

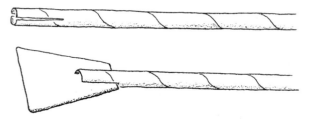

Form the letters N, S, E and W from pieces of wire or unbent paper clips. Wind them around the pencil, one inch below the arrow. Prop the pencil up by its point in a lump of clay, in the earth of a shallow flowerpot, or even in a plastic container filled with nails or something else to weigh it down.

Place the weather vane in a place where the wind is not blocked by buildings. Use a compass to make sure your NSEW letters are set up correctly.

What happens:
As the wind blows, the weather vane moves.

Why:
When the wind blows, it pushes away the larger surface (the arrow). As a result, the other end points into the wind, in the direction from which the wind is blowing.

In the Northern Hemisphere, a wind that shifts in a counterclockwise direction usually brings a low pressure system and stormy weather along with it. East winds generally bring rain, west winds clearing. North winds mean cold weather, and south winds heat. In the Southern Hemisphere, it is exactly the opposite for every direction.

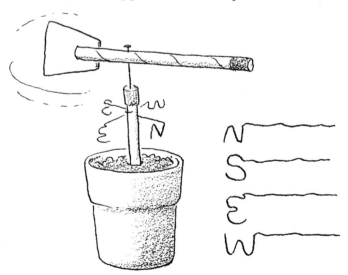

Cup Anemometer

How can you measure the speed of wind? One way is with a cup anemometer. This instrument has three or four small hollow metal hemispheres that revolve around a metal rod and catch the wind. How fast they move reveals the speed of the wind. Our anemometer looks almost like the real thing. But while real anemometers record the revolutions of the cups electrically, we have to count them ourselves.

You need:

2 pieces of a heavy
    cardboard
    or a corrugated box
scissors
staples or tacks
4 individual metal-foil
    muffin pans
paint

large needle or
    sharp, thin nail
pencil with eraser
clay or paper towels
glue or cord
block of wood or
    flat stone

What to do:

Cut out two strips of heavy cardboard, approximately 2″×18″ (5cm × 45cm). Make a slit in the middle of each one so that they fit together to make a cross. Staple a small metal-foil pan to each end of the cross. If you don't have any old muffin

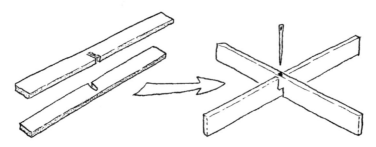

pans around, you can make them by cutting out disks from heavy duty aluminum foil, or cutting down paper cups. Paint one of the pans a bright color. Make a hole through the center of the cross with a sharp thin nail or a large needle.

To make a base, stick the eye of a needle into a pencil eraser. Fit the pointed end of the pencil into the hole of a spool. (You may need clay or paper towels to make it snug.) Glue or tie the spool to a block of wood or a flat stone.

Attach the cross to the base by placing it on the point of the needle. Blow on the cups. If the cross does not turn easily, make the hole in the crossed strips larger.

Place the base outdoors on a box about three feet above the ground. Keep a record of the number of revolutions per minute. You can do this easily by counting how many times the colored pan passes you.

What happens:

The anemometer sometimes whirls around very quickly. At other times it barely moves.

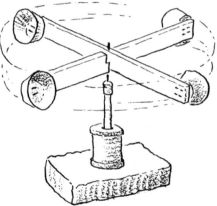

Why:

The inward curve of the cups receives most of the force of the wind. That's what makes the cups move. The more revolutions per minute, the greater the wind velocity. A rapid increase in speed can mean approaching rain or snow or thunderstorms.

THE BEAUFORT SCALE

The Beaufort scale was originally designed by Francis Beaufort, a British admiral, in the early 1800s to help guide ships. It calculated wind speed at sea, but it has since been adapted for use on land. The Weather Bureau, though it uses an anemometer to measure wind speed, still reports winds to us using the Beaufort Scale.

It gives you a great way to judge the speed of wind—anywhere, anytime—by watching the things that the wind moves. Memorize it and you'll be able to amaze people with your accurate readings.

Beaufort Scale #	Description	Effect on land	Wind Speed MPH
0	calm	Smoke goes straight up	less than 1
1	light air	Smoke drifts in direction of wind	1–3
2	light breeze	Wind felt on face; leaves rustle; flags stir; weather vanes turn	4–7
3	gentle breeze	Leaves and twigs move constantly; light flags blow out	8–12
4	moderate breeze	Dust, loose papers, and small branches move; flags flap	13–18

5		fresh breeze	Small trees in leaf begin to sway; flags ripple	19–24
6		strong breeze	Large branches in motion; flags beat; umbrellas turn inside out	25–31
7		moderate gale	Whole trees in motion; flags are extended	32–38
8		fresh gale	Twigs break off trees; walking is hard	39–46
9		strong gale	Slight damage to houses—TV antennas may blow off, awnings rip	47–54
10		whole gale	Trees uprooted; much damage to houses	55–63
11		storm	Widespread damage	64–75
12		hurricane	Excessive damage	more than 75

HOW COLD DO YOU FEEL?

The speed of wind affects how cold we feel.

The wind-chill factor is the relationship between the speed of wind and the temperature of the air. A wind chill table tells us the still-air temperature that would feel the same as the temperature and wind speed combined. For instance, a temperature of 20°F(-6°C) and a wind of 20 miles an hour (32km) makes us feel as though it were -10°F (-23°C).

Wind Chill Table

AIR TEMPERATURE (°F)

WIND SPEED (MILES PER HOUR)	35	30	25	20	15	10	5	0	−5	−10	−15	−20	−25	−30	−35	−40	−45
0–4	35	30	25	20	15	10	5	0	−5	−10	−15	−20	−25	−30	−35	−40	−45
5	32	27	22	16	11	6	0	−5	−10	−15	−21	−26	−31	−36	−42	−47	−52
10	22	16	10	3	−3	−9	−15	−22	−27	−34	−40	−46	−52	−58	−64	−71	−77
15	16	9	2	−5	−11	−18	−25	−31	−38	−45	−51	−58	−65	−72	−78	−85	−92
20	12	4	−3	−10	−17	−24	−31	−39	−46	−53	−60	−67	−74	−81	−88	−95	−103
25	8	1	−7	−15	−22	−29	−36	−44	−51	−59	−66	−74	−81	−88	−96	−103	−110
30	6	−2	−10	−18	−25	−33	−41	−49	−56	−64	−71	−79	−86	−93	−101	−109	−116
35	4	−4	−12	−20	−27	−35	−43	−52	−58	−67	−74	−82	−89	−97	−105	−113	−120
40	3	−5	−13	−21	−29	−37	−45	−53	−60	−69	−76	−84	−92	−100	−107	−115	−123
45	2	−6	−14	−22	−30	−38	−46	−54	−62	−70	−78	−85	−93	−102	−109	−117	−125

WIND SPEEDS GREATER THAN 40 MPH HAVE LITTLE ADDITIONAL CHILLING EFFECT

To convert miles to kilometers, multiply miles by 1.6. To convert Fahrenheit to Centigrade, see the instructions on page 98.

Milk Carton Hygrometer

Humidity is the amount of water vapor (moisture) in the air. Meteorologists don't usually report actual humidity to us, however, but what is called "relative humidity." That's a figure they come to by comparing the moisture in the air to the amount of moisture that the air can hold. And that amount will change according to the temperature of the air. High humidity combined with high temperatures makes most people uncomfortable.

You can figure out the relative humidity with a homemade hygrometer.

You need:

2 room thermometers	a quart milk carton
small piece of	rubber bands
cotton material	scissors
thread	

What to do:

Check the two thermometers to make sure they register the same temperature.

Cover the bulb of one of the thermometers with a two-inch scrap of cotton material (an old handkerchief will do fine). Tie it on with thread or string, and leave a "tail" on one end, as in the illustration.

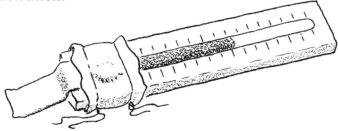

If you have an old cotton shoelace, you can use that instead. Just slip the bulb into the fabric tube and secure it with string.

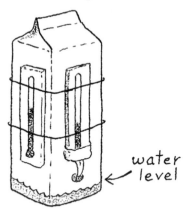

Using rubber bands, attach the thermometers to two sides of a milk carton. Cut a small hole in the carton just below the thermometer with the covered bulb. Push the tail of cotton through the hole. Fill the carton with water up to the level of the hole so you can keep the cotton wet.

Read the dry bulb and wet bulb thermometers.

What happens:
The temperature of the wet-bulb thermometer is always lower.

Why:
Water evaporating from the thermometer with the moist cloth uses up heat. Therefore, the temperature drops.

The water in the cloth around the wet-bulb thermometer will keep on evaporating as long as the air can hold more water vapor. Dry air can take on more water vapor than air that is already filled with moisture.

112

The drier the air (the lower the humidity), the further apart the two temperature readings will be. When the temperatures are exactly the same, the humidity is 100 per cent.

The higher the temperature, the more water vapor the air can hold. When the air has as much water vapor as it can hold at a particular temperature, the relative humidity is 100 per cent. And it is foggy or raining or snowing.

Check the readings of the two thermometers and see the humidity table (below) to find the relative percentage of humidity.

Relative Humidity Table

DIFFERENCE BETWEEN DRY-BULB AND WET-BULB TEMPERATURES

DRY-BULB TEMPERATURE (°F)	1	2	3	4	5	6	7	8	9	10	11	12	14	16	18	20	22	24
10	78	56	34	13														
15	82	64	46	29	11													
20	85	70	55	40	26	12												
25	87	74	62	49	37	25	13	1										
30	89	78	67	56	46	36	26	16	6									
35	91	81	72	63	54	45	36	27	19	10	2							
40	92	83	75	68	60	52	45	37	29	22	15	7						
45	93	86	78	71	64	57	51	44	38	31	25	18	6					
50	93	87	80	74	67	61	55	49	43	38	32	27	16	5				
55	94	88	82	76	70	65	59	54	49	43	38	33	23	14	5			
60	94	89	83	78	73	68	63	58	53	48	43	39	30	21	13	5		
65	95	90	85	80	75	70	66	61	56	52	48	44	35	27	20	12	5	
70	95	90	86	81	77	72	68	64	59	55	51	48	40	33	25	19	12	6
75	96	91	86	82	78	74	70	66	62	58	54	51	44	37	30	24	18	12
80	96	91	87	83	79	75	72	68	64	61	57	54	47	41	35	29	23	18
90	96	92	89	85	81	78	74	71	68	65	61	58	52	47	41	36	31	26
100	96	93	89	86	83	80	77	73	70	68	65	62	56	51	46	41	37	33

Example: If the dry bulb temperature is 65 (see numbers at left), and the wet bulb temperature is 62, the difference is 3 degrees (see numbers at the top of the chart), and so the relative humidity is 85% (see the place where they intersect).

HOW HOT DO YOU FEEL?

It's 85°F (29.4°C). How hot do you feel?

Well, if the humidity is 95 per cent—it feels like 105°F (40.5°C). The Heat Index prepared by the weather service shows what the temperature feels like as the humidity changes.

At 110°F (43°C), you only need relative humidity of 50 per cent to feel as if the temperature is 150°F (65°C)!

With the hygrometer, the relative humidity chart, and this index, you can figure out how hot it feels any day.

Heat Index

RELATIVE HUMIDITY(%)

AIR TEMPERATURE (°F)	25	30	35	40	45	50	55	60	65	70	75	80	85	90	95	100
140																
135																
130																
125																
120	139	148														
115	127	135	143	151												
110	117	123	130	137	143	150										
105	109	113	118	123	129	135	142	149								
100	101	104	107	110	115	120	126	132	138	144						
95	94	96	98	101	104	107	110	114	119	124	130	136				
90	88	90	91	93	95	96	98	100	102	106	109	113	117	122		
85	83	84	85	86	87	88	89	90	91	93	95	97	99	102	105	108
80	77	78	79	79	80	81	81	82	83	85	86	86	87	88	89	91
75	72	73	73	74	74	75	75	76	76	77	77	78	78	79	79	80
70	66	67	67	68	68	69	69	70	70	70	70	71	71	71	71	72

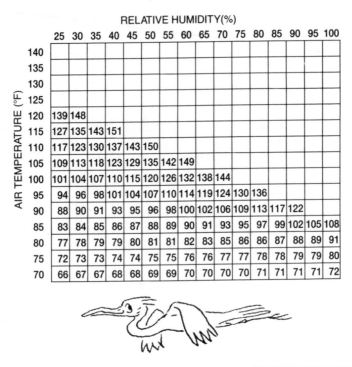

HOW UNCOMFORTABLE DO YOU FEEL?

The Temperature Humidity Index (THI) shows how heat and humidity combined make us feel.

If you know the temperature and the relative humidity, you can use the chart below and tell just how uncomfortable you are!

Temperature Humidity Index

PERCENT RELATIVE HUMIDITY

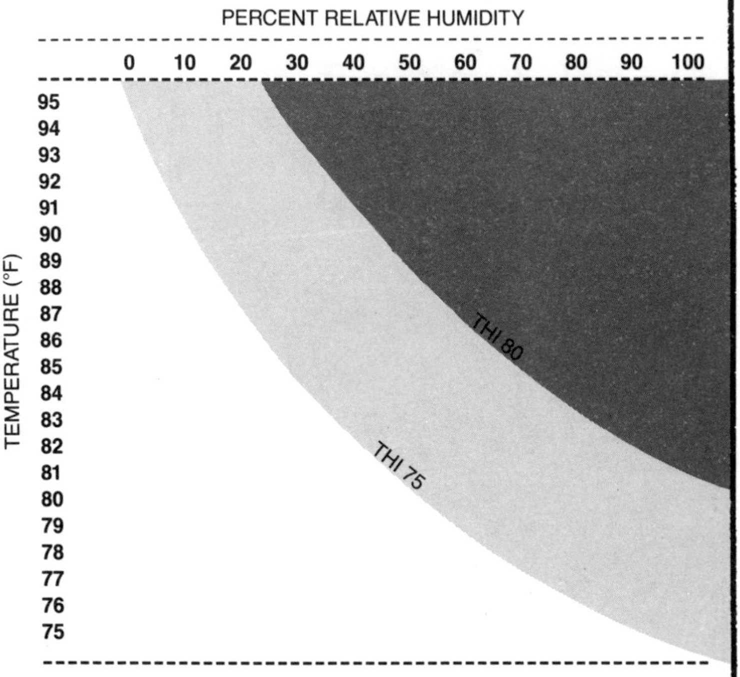

For example, if the temperature is 81°F (27.2°C) with the humidity at 55 per cent, the THI is 75, and about half the people are uncomfortable. At that same temperature and a humidity of 100 per cent, the THI is 80 and most people are uncomfortable.

If you love math, you can figure out the THI for yourself by using the following steps:

    1. Add the wet bulb and dry bulb temperatures.

    2. Multiply the sum by 0.4.

    3. Add 15.

If you don't have the wet bulb temperature, but you know the temperature and the humidity, you can find the wet bulb temperature by using the relative humidity table on page 109. All you have to do is subtract the "difference" from the dry bulb temperature.

Dew Point

The dew point is the temperature at which the air can't hold any more water vapor. That's when the moisture in the air begins to condense—to turn back from water vapor to droplets. This temperature will change from day to day depending on the temperature of the air and the amount of moisture in it. The closer the dew point temperature is to the air temperature, the more likely we are to have fog or rain or snow.

You can use simple equipment to determine the day's dew point, but you need to set it up outdoors.

You need:
a can   a thermometer
water   ice cubes

What to do:
Jot down the temperature of the air.

Remove the label from an ordinary metal can. Fill the can with water, and then make sure the outside is dry. Place the thermometer in the can.

Add ice to the water, a little at a time. Carefully stir it with the thermometer. Watch both the outside of the can and the thermometer closely.

What happens:
Liquid begins to form on the outside of the can—and the temperature goes down.

Why:
The temperature—at the point when liquid begins to form—is at or near the dew point—the temperature at which relative humidity is 100 percent.

When water cools off and condenses on an object, the droplets are called dew. Dew forms when damp air touches anything that cools it to below its dew point—the point at which it cannot hold any more water.

When air currents are rising rapidly, cooling takes place high in the air and clouds form. When gentler air currents mix cool air into warmer air, fog forms.

Dew usually forms on grass or on plants that have cooled off. The temperature at which this happens depends on the amount of water vapor in the air. If it's small, dew may not form until the temperature drops to 32°F (0°C) or even below freezing. When it's that cold, frost forms. If the air contains a great deal of water vapor, dew will form at 68°F (20°C).

Rain Gauge

Measure the amount of rain that falls during a period of a week or month, and compare your results with the official statistics.

You need:

various containers (a coffee can, a jar, a cut down milk carton)

masking tape
a ruler

What to do:

Using a ruler, measure off inches or centimeters on strips of masking or adhesive tape. Attach the tapes to the various containers.

Put the containers in a flat, level open place. A windowsill will do fine. (It may be wise to place them in a box to make sure they remain upright.)

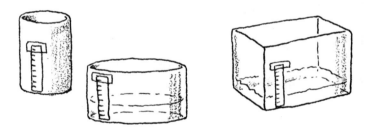

Each time it rains, measure the amount of rain in the containers. The levels should be the same whatever the size of the container, provided that its sides are parallel. Record the amount and date.

Compare measurements from one rainfall to the next. And compare your measurements with those announced on TV or radio. They may not always agree. Sometimes, the amount of rain varies from one side of the street to the other!

READING THE CLOUDS

When the air is heavy with moisture and it gets cool, the water vapor in it turns back into droplets and combines with tiny dust particles in the air to form fog. When fog is high in the sky, we see clouds. The type of cloud depends on how the air is cooled and the way the air is moving.

Cirrus clouds are high, feathery clouds.

Stratus clouds hang low in layers or sheets in the sky, causing overcast and fog.

Cumulus clouds look like cauliflowers with flat bases. They usually mean fair weather.

Nimbus clouds are dark gray rain clouds.

Most clouds change shape continually. Parts of them evaporate when touched by warmer air and when winds blow.

Weather is called cloudless when there are no clouds at all, and "clear" when clouds cover less than $3/10$ of the sky. It is "partly sunny" when the key is $3/10$-$7/10$ clouded, and "cloudy" or overcast when more than that.

Weather forecasters study clouds carefully. With the help of the Cloud Chart, you, too, can read the clouds!

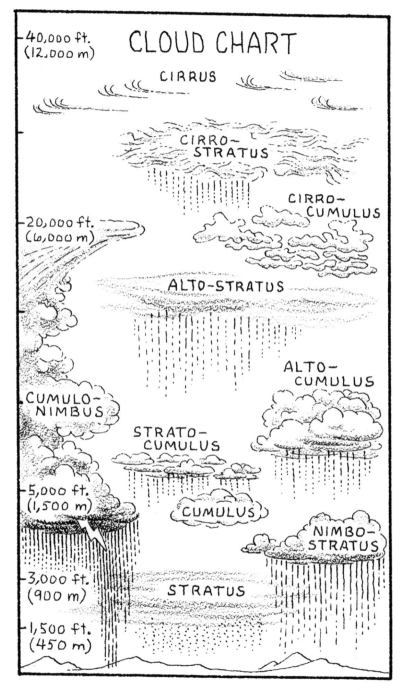

CLOUD CHART

pH Scale

The pH scale, developed by S.P.L. Sorensen, a Danish biochemist, is used to indicate how alkaline or acid a solution is.

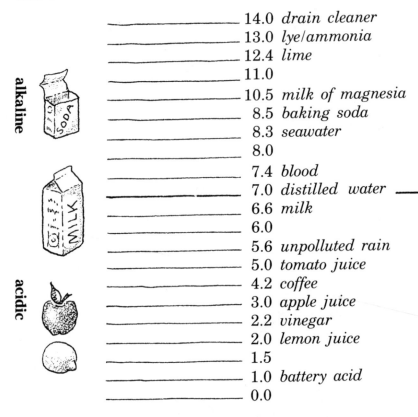

	14.0	*drain cleaner*
	13.0	*lye/ammonia*
	12.4	*lime*
	11.0	
	10.5	*milk of magnesia*
	8.5	*baking soda*
	8.3	*seawater*
	8.0	
	7.4	*blood*
	7.0	*distilled water*
	6.6	*milk*
	6.0	
	5.6	*unpolluted rain*
	5.0	*tomato juice*
	4.2	*coffee*
	3.0	*apple juice*
	2.2	*vinegar*
	2.0	*lemon juice*
	1.5	
	1.0	*battery acid*
	0.0	

alkaline / acidic

All acids contain hydrogen. The stronger the acid, the more hydrogen the solution contains—and the less hydrogen the solution can accept when it combines with another substance. When it can't accept any more hydrogen its ph is 0. The stronger the acid, the lower its pH.

A solution with a pH above 7 is alkaline. A solution with a pH below 7 is acid.

Acid Rain

You can test whether the rain that falls in your area is polluted by using pH paper or litmus paper, both of which you can buy from chemistry laboratories or hobby shops. Or you can make your own indicator with juice from a jar of red cabbage.

You need:

6–10 tablespoons of red cabbage juice (75–125mL)
5 small glasses or paper cups
rainwater
apple juice
lemon juice
a clean jar
cooled boiled water
milk

What to do:

Collect rainwater in a clean jar.

Line up and number or label the paper cups. Put a tablespoon of red cabbage juice in each. Add rainwater to the first, an equal amount of cooled boiled water to the second, milk to the third, apple juice to the next, then lemon juice to the last.

Compare the color of the cup with the rainwater with the colors of others. When you find the one that comes closest in color to the rainwater, refer to the pH chart and estimate the pH of the rainwater you are testing.

What happens:

If the solution changes color only slightly, your rainwater is normal. If it becomes as pink as the lemon solution, it has a very high acid content.

Why:

Rain is normally slightly acidic because of the oxides in the air that form weak acids. Unpolluted rainwater measures about 5.6 on the pH scale.

If your rainwater has a lower pH level, the rain falling in your area is polluted with acids. When the pH of water in lakes and streams drops below 5 on the scale, most fish die.

When the waste from the fuel burned to run our factories—and our cars, trains and planes—combines with the water in the air, it forms acids that fall to the ground—either in the form of rain or as dry particles.

This new man-made pollution has been called a slow poison from the sky. It harms trees and food crops, and poses a threat to life in lakes and streams, as well on land. It can even crumble buildings.

Weather Glossary

acid rain—air pollution formed by the reaction of water in the air with chemicals, particularly sulfur dioxide, given off as waste, mostly by factories and automobiles

air mass—a body of air hundreds or thousands of miles across with the same temperature and moisture

anemometer—an instrument for measuring wind speed

atmosphere—the air surrounding the Earth

Ballot's Law—the relationship between the direction of the wind and the location of the high and low pressure areas making it

barometer—an instrument for measuring air pressure

Beaufort Scale—a measure of wind strength

condensation—change of a substance from a gas to a liquid

Coriolis effect—the apparent force that as a result of the Earth's rotation deflects air currents to the right in the Northern Hemisphere and to the left in the Southern Hemisphere

dew point—the temperature at which air is saturated with water and water vapor condenses

electromagnetic spectrum—the range of wavelengths of radiation from the Sun, extending from gamma rays to radio waves (and including x-rays, ultraviolet, visible light and infrared rays)

eye of a hurricane—area of relative calm at the center of a hurricane

front—boundary between cold and warm air masses, usually represented on weather map with an "L", because it forms a low pressure center

greenhouse effect—the warming of the lower layers of the atmosphere caused by heat being trapped by increased carbon dioxide in the air

high—higher than normal air pressure, such as the surface pressure at the center of an air mass. Represented on a weather map with an "H"

hurricane—a cyclonic storm, usually tropical in origin. Called cyclone in the Indian Ocean, typhoon in the Pacific, and willy-willy in Australia

hygrometer—an instrument for measuring moisture in the air

jet stream—high speed winds above the stratosphere usually blowing in a westerly direction

low—lower than normal air pressure, such as the boundary between air masses. Represented on a weather map by "L", it usually means bad weather.

meteorologist—a scientist who studies weather and climate

millibar—a unit of atmospheric pressure used by meteorologists (1 inch = 33.87 millibars)

ozone—a special form of oxygen (with 3 atoms) that forms naturally in the upper air and filters out the Sun's harmful ultraviolet rays. In the lower air it contributes to smog.

precipitation—water that falls from the clouds to earth as rain, snow, sleet, or hail

prevailing winds—winds that usually blow from the same direction

relative humidity—the amount of moisture in the air compared to the moisture that the air can hold at that particular temperature

station model—a weather report using picture symbols to indicate the various weather factors

stratosphere—the lower part of the atmosphere in which most weather takes place

temperature-humidity index—a chart that measures the discomfort we feel based on a combination of temperature and moisture in the air

tornado—a violent, whirling wind along with a funnel-shaped cloud. Also known as a twister

updraft—a column of air moving rapidly upward inside a storm

water cycle—the process by which oceans and smaller bodies of water evaporate into the air and then condense and return in the form of rain or snow

wind chill factor—a measure of the discomfort we feel based on a combination of temperature and wind speed

Index

Acid rain, 123
Acid solution, 122
Agata, Siberia, 99
Air, 43–47
    mass, 56–57
    pollution, 39, 49, 50
    pressure, 58–59, 101–102
Alkaline solutions, 122
Anemometer, 106–107, 108
Aneroid barometer, 99, 103
Antarctica, 9, 41, 82
Arica, Chile, 69
Assam, India, 69
Atacama, Chile, 69
Atmosphere, 30, 40, 42
Atmospheric pressure, measuring,
    100
Autumn, 22–23
Azizia, Tripolitania, 9

Ballot's Law, 61
Bangladesh, 41
Barometer
    aneroid, 99, 103
    balloon, 102–103
    bottle, 100–101
    reading a, 99
Barometric pressure, 99
Beaufort Scale, 108–109
Bernoulli's Law, 64–65
Breezes, sea, 54

Cancer, skin, 82
Carbon: dioxide, 39; monoxide, 49
Celsius, Anders, 97
Centigrade, converting from
    Fahrenheit to, 98
Central keys, Florida, 41
Centrifugal force, 66
Chinook, 54
Chlorofluorocarbons, 82
Clouds, 77–80, 120; chart, 121
Cockeyed Bob, 54
Coffeyville, Kansas, 85
Colors, 78, 92–93
Commonwealth Bay, Antarctica, 41
Condensation, 76
Converting miles to kilometers, 110
Coriolis effect, 52
Cup anemometer, 106–107
Cyclones, 65, 67

Dallol, Ethiopia, 9

Day and night, 26
Death Valley, California, 9
Dew Point, 117
Drizzle, 80

Electricity, 86–87
Electromagnetic spectrum, 125
Ellipse, 32, 37
Energy, 11, 12
Equator, 20
Evaporation, 70, 73, 76
Exosphere, 42
Eye of the hurricane, 66, 67

Fahrenheit, Gabriel, 97
Fahrenheit, converting from
    Centigrade to, 98
Fog, 118
Foehn, 54
Foucault, Jean Bernard Leon, 28
Fronts, 56, 57
Frost, 84, 118

Galileo Galilei, 97
Greenhouse effect, 38

Hail, 80, 84–85
Heat, 6–39
Helium, 11
Helm winds, 54
Highs, 124
Hot spell, longest, 9
Humidity, 70, 112; *also see* Relative
    humidity, THI
Hurricane, 66, 67
Hurricane, eye of, 66–67
    worst, 41
Hydrocarbons, 82
Hydrogen, 122
Hygrometer, 74, 111

Inversion, air, 48–49

Java, Indonesia, 69
Jet streams, 55

Kauai, Hawaii, 69

Le Reunion, 69
Lighting, 86–91

Martin Bar, Western Australia, 9
Mercury, 97, 99, 100
Mesopause, 42

Mesosphere, 42
Milk carton hygrometer, 111
Millibars, 95, 99
Mistral, 54–55
Monsoons, 55
Mt. Shasta, California, 69
Mt. Washington,
    New Hampshire, 41

Night and day, 26
Nitrogen, 47
    acids, 82
North Pole, 20–21

Oxygen, 47, 82
Oymyakon, Siberia, 9
Ozone, 82

Pantheon, 28
Pendulum, 18
pH scale, 122
Pleasteau Station, Antarctica, 9
Pollution, 81–82, 124
    air, 49–50
Precipitation records, 69
Pressure, air, 58–59
Puelche, 54

Radiant energy, 12
Rain, 79, 107
    acid, 123–124
    drops, 80
    gauge, 119
Rainbow, 92–93
Rainfall, 69
Records
    keeping, 95
    precipitation, 69
    weather, 9
    wind, 41
Relative humidity, 111–113
Rotation, Earth's, 25–27
Rust, 47

Seasons, 34–36
Shadow
    length, 23, 24
    thermometer, 22–23
Silver Lake, Colorado, 69
Simoons, 55
Sleet, 83, 84
Slope winds, 54
Smog, 81
Smoke, 49

Snow, 15, 69, 83, 107
Sorenson, S.P.L., 122
Squall, 54
Spectrum, 93
Station model, 95
Storm, how far away it is, 91
Storm warnings, 88–89
Stratopause, 42
Stratosphere, 42, 82
Straw thermometer, 96–97
Sulphur dioxide, 49
Summer, 17–19
Sun, 10–12, 18, 19, 21, 22–23, 26–27,
    30–31, 78

Temperature, 13–15
    Conversion Chart, 98
    converting Fahrenheit and
        Centigrade, 98
    Humidity Index, 115
    records, 9
THI, 115
Thermometer, straw, 96–97
Thermosphere, 42
Thunder, 90–91
    storms, 88, 107
Tornado, 62–65
    records, 41
Torricelli, Evangelista, 100
Tropopause, 42
Troposphere, 126
Twisters, 67
Typhoons, 67

Ultraviolet rays, 82
Updraft, 67

Vostok, Antarctica, 9

Warnings, storm, 88–89
Water, 68–93
    cycle, 124
Weather station instruments, 94–124
Weather vane, 104–105
Wichita Falls, Texas, 41
Williwaw, 54
Willy-willies, 67
Wind, 39–68
    chill factor, 110
    records, 41
    speed of, 106–110
Winter, 17–19

Zondas, 54